The Lost

Phil Grabsky

Temple of Java

SEVEN DIALS

For Joe, Eddie and the wee'un —
I hope places like Borobudur are still there when you grow up.

First published in the United Kingdom in
1999 by Orion

This paperback edition first published
in 2000 by
Seven Dials, Cassell & Co
Wellington House, 125 Strand
London, WC2R 0BB

Text copyright
© Phil Grabsky/Seventh Art

Phil Grabsky/Seventh Art has asserted
the right to be identified as the author
of this work.

All rights reserved. No part of this
publication may be reproduced in any
material form (including photocopying
or storing it in any medium by electronic
means and whether or not transiently
or incidentally to some other use of
this publication) without the written
permission of the copyright owner.

Distributed in the USA by
Sterling Publishing Co., Inc.
387 Park Avenue South,
New York, NY 10016-8810

A CIP catalogue record for this book is
available from the British Library
ISBN 1 84188 058 2

Printed and bound by Butler and Tanner
Ltd., Frome, England

ACKNOWLEDGEMENTS

Without the commitment and dedication of certain
individuals at the BBC, there would be no book and
no accompanying TV film. Things are changing, so
enjoy the BBC while you can. Particular thanks are
due to Laurence Rees, series editor of the history
series 'TimeWatch'. His confidence in me and
Seventh Art Productions is appreciated as are his
encouragement and valuable advice throughout the
film-making process. I would like to stress how
indebted I am to Mehreen Saigol, my researcher who
worked tirelessly and diligently. Thanks also to all the
consultants – Nigel Barley, John Villiers, Roy Jordaan,
Adji Damais, and, above all, John Miksic. At Seventh
Art, I could not have made the film without Head of
Production and partner, Amanda Wilkie. And how
fortunate I feel to have once again worked with the
talents of cameraman Jonathan Patridge and sound
recordist Simon Farmer. Credit is also due to Michael
O'Donoghue, McDonald Brown, Dimo Tchamouroff,
Matt Skilton, Cliff and Mike Barton, Tim and Maya
Byard-Jones, Eko Binarso and Cip in Java.

As regards this book, my thanks go to Trevor Dolby
at Orion for seeing the whole thing through.

Finally, gratitude is due to the monks at Mendut
Monastery, alongside Borobudur, for being so calm,
kind and caring. They set an example to us all.

CONTENTS

T'AI-WAN
(TAIWAN)

SIAM
(THAILAND)

GREAT VIETNAM
(VIETNAM)

SOUTH
CHINA
SEA

CAMBODIA

Manila •

P H I L I P P I N E S

• *Saigon*

Penang •

M A L A Y A

Brunei •
(Bandar Sen Begawan)

Malacca •
(Kuala Lumpur)

Johore
• (Singapore)

S U M A T R A

B O R N E O

C E L E B E S
(SULAWESI)

• *Jambi*

Makassar •
(Ujung Panclang)

Batavia
• (Jakarta)

J A V A

Surabaya
(Surabaia)

Borobudur

BALI

T I M O R

I N D I A N

O C E A N

0   500   1000 *MILES*

$P\ A\ C\ I\ F\ I\ C \quad O\ C\ E\ A\ N$

MOLUCCAS

NEW
GUINEA

ARAFURA SEA

AUSTRALIA

PART 1

Borobudur

In front of me, one of the 72 stupas
had been stripped of its outer casing,
revealing the Buddha – serene in
contemplation of the new dawn.
The volcanic andesite from which it
is made is relatively easy to work and
not at all a smooth compact stone like
marble. But the skill of the sculpture
gave it a grace that was quite breath-
taking. For a thousand years, this and
the other 503 Buddhas on the temple
have been at one with their place, their
temple and their land. In the still blue
light, it was impossible not to feel an
enormous sense of calm and peace.

1

DAWN ON THE TEMPLE

4.15 A.M. 27TH MAY.

I had never heard of Borobudur until a few months earlier, and now I was about to see dawn rise above what some have called the most beautiful building in Southeast Asia. As a film-maker I have been privileged to travel to some truly awe-inspiring sites throughout the world from Mexico to Libya, India to South Africa. But the thrill of discovery is no less powerful for having been awestruck before. I couldn't wait, therefore, to see Borobudur. The drive from the hotel in the nearby town of Yogyakarta took 45 minutes through the dark. Passing the numerous souvenir shops – already wakening in preparation for today's slice of its million tourists a year – I came to a perimeter fence and gate. I still couldn't see the monument and began to wonder whether the tales of its size and majesty had been exaggerated. Once inside, torch in hand, I made my way along a trail. Sunrise was only ten or twenty minutes away, and the sky was beginning to redden. I turned a corner and there it was – Borobudur. I admit that I had steeled myself to be disappointed – I had a 50-minute film to make for the BBC and I was concerned that the temple actually might not justify such an amount of time. The only illumination was some variously coloured spotlights, but they were sufficient enough to stop me in my tracks. What I saw before me was enormous, ambitious, proud and graceful.

I hurried closer, feeling increasingly humble. My aim was to go straight to the top and watch the sun rise. I already knew that this was not the way the temple was supposed to be used but, after all, I was a tourist. The stairs through the seven terraces are steep and, even before Java's hot and humid day begins, they demand a certain exertion. Deliberately trying not to look around too much, I climbed straight to the central stupa and sat looking east.

Borobudur is an extraordinary construction of 1.6 million blocks of volcanic andesite. There are four square terraces, three circular ones and a central stupa at the top.

So close to the equator, the days are regular – more or less 6 a.m. to 6 p.m. And sunrise and sunset happen before your eyes. You can clearly see the light changing from black to deep blue, to sky blue. Directly ahead of me to the east was the volcano called Merapi, one of the most active volcanoes on earth. Slowly its smoke could be seen outlined against the sky. Magically the sun rose directly behind the mountain. And as the light spread, I – alone on the summit of the temple – could look around me. I felt as if I had landed in an entirely alien environment. Bell-shaped stupas, perforated and, I already knew, containing seated Buddhas, surrounded me. I had never seen anything like it. In front of me, one of the 72 stupas had been stripped of its outer casing, revealing the Buddha – serene in contemplation of the new dawn. The volcanic andesite from which it is made is relatively easy to work and not at all a smooth compact stone like marble. But the skill of the sculpture gave it a grace that was quite breath-taking. For a thousand years, this and the other 503 Buddhas on the temple have been at one with their place, their temple and their land. In the still blue light, it was impossible not to feel an enormous sense of calm and peace.

I had been trying to take notes and record light changes on my small video camera, but I had to keep stopping, simply to observe the light changing on the stone. I had not realized that grey could contain so much variation and could visibly alter so quickly. I saw orange, blue, pale blue, green – all simple washes across the stone as the sun made its swift ascent. As the sun rose, so the temperature increased and the humidity began. The stones began to feel warm as if they too had had new life breathed into them. What, I wondered, could Thomas Stamford Raffles, the man credited with rediscovering the temple, have possibly thought when he saw this for the first time? He had not seen the pyramids, the Colosseum, the Acropolis. Borobudur therefore must have been even more staggering to this inquisitive employee of the British East India Company. And what must the original pilgrims have thought, a thousand years ago, heaving their way across the hills and mountains, through swamp and jungle, to reach here? What must have been their reaction when they crossed the last mountain pass and saw the temple sitting in the volcanic plain before them? Here was a building the size of which, the shape of which, the colour of which they would never have even dreamt of. In a world of wooden buildings and green fields, Borobudur would have struck them as utterly extraordinary, if not alien – of another world, of the gods.

Laden with notebook, guidebooks, camera and water bottle, I couldn't hope to understand the depth of ancient impressions, but I had not been disappointed by my own. Impressive though it is to hear about a million and a half blocks of stone, approximately three miles of reliefs about a temple that took decades to build, what was clearly even more impressive was the sense of an ancient people and their craft, their culture, their undoubted pride in something quite magnificent.

6.20 a.m. The park's PA system had announced that the gates were open and normal tourist hours had been resumed. Within a few minutes the first bus disgorged Spanish and Italian tourists who slowly began their own ascent, chattering and laughing their way to the top. One left her chewing gum on a wall without a thought. From another stairwell a group of elderly Indonesians appeared and rushed to put their hands through one of the perforated stupas to touch the Buddha for luck. Then small groups of Indonesian youths arrived. Some were shyly courting and simply wished to hold hands, others were English students and wanted to talk to the tourists. I admired their enthusiasm to be either courting or studying at 6.30 in the morning.

By 7 a.m. the top was awash with people. The noise was tremendous – cameras, cassette players, laughter. The sounds of the plain were equally audible – motorbikes, calls to prayer, children crying, loud music. This was a living monument in a real world. Indeed it is Indonesia's most popular site and it sounded as if most of the country had chosen this morning to visit.

Throughout it all sat the Buddhas. Eyes closed in contemplation. Legs crossed. Hands symbolically placed. Poised, elegant, humble.

2

THE EIGHTH WONDER OF THE WORLD

Borobudur? The name is unfamiliar, the spelling foreign and strange. And yet Borobudur is, without question, one of the wonders of the world. In the second century BC a Greek historian named Antipatros wrote a list of the seven greatest wonders of the ancient world. These were places chosen not only for their appearance but also for the purpose and imagination that lay behind them. These sites – the Pharos of Alexandria, the Great Pyramid, the Hanging Gardens of Babylon, the temple of Artemis, the Colossus of Rhodes, the Statue of Zeus and the Mausoleum of Halicarnassus – were considered at the time as being without equal. Sadly, only the Pyramid still stands, so we cannot see for ourselves the choice Antipatros made. The other six have crumbled and largely returned to the dust from which they were originally sculptured. Over the past 2000 years, how many of mankind's greatest wonders have met a similar fate? Those that have survived have often done so through the good fortune of having been abandoned, somewhat off the main routes and thoroughfares. Slowly enveloped by tree and bush or covered by ash and sand, some buildings have survived the centuries. The work of archaeologists and explorers during the last 200 years has uncovered many of these hidden wonders. Some have been called the 'eighth wonder' of the world. And one such claimant, with a case as good as any and better than most, is Borobudur – the lost temple of Java.

Its 1.6 million blocks of worked volcanic stone comprise perhaps the most creatively lavish building in history. Its 1460 reliefs, each one with a different personality, cover three miles of wall. From square lower terraces to circular upper ones, the building forms something entirely unique – there is nothing like it anywhere else on earth. And yet, for over a thousand years, it was obscured, ignored, lost in a jungle of palm and plant. Not until 1814 and the arrival of an

Englishman, Thomas Stamford Raffles, was the temple rediscovered and rejuvenated. The lost temple had been found.

Buildings such as this will never be built again, and history is littered with examples of their destruction and pillaging. It is our good fortune that the temple was, it seems, hastily abandoned in the early 900s and slowly left to the foliage around it. Why a building that had taken probably 60 or 70 years to build was then left after only another 60 or 70 years has been one of its mysteries. But its slow reabsorption into the countryside saved it from the possibility of human vandalism. Yet nature too can be just as effective at ruin, and Raffles' own commissioned drawings of the site show how close to collapse it had become. Once again, we are fortunate that Raffles was an enlightened individual who, rather than stripping the monument of its finest works, and leaving the rest to crumble, set about clearing the site and where possible restoring it. His example proved decisive, and in the two centuries since the rediscovery, the temple has seen intermittent but determined attempts to restore it to its original beauty and grace. Dutch endeavours in the nineteenth and twentieth centuries and a UNESCO-sponsored attempt between 1973 and 1983 have resulted in the building being restored to something like its past glory. In the case of the UNESCO project, a million blocks were numbered, taken down, treated, dried and laboriously reinstated. It was a remarkable feat of energy and engineering which has secured the future of Borobudur for centuries to come. It also allowed some of the same questions that occurred to Raffles when he first saw the temple to be re-evaluated and answered afresh.

Much concerning Borobudur is open to debate. It is mysterious, contradictory and confusing. The peoples who built it left few inscriptions. There is no dedication on even one of those many stones. Any written texts, having been scribed on to palm leaves, have decayed. Few travellers left reports; in China, for example, only monks were allowed to travel at this time, and we have few eyewitness accounts on their part. Judging by the absence of factual travelogues, it seems few Indians came this way either – and, of course, absolutely no Europeans. Much must be deduced from the very stone and soil that make up Borobudur. This is what Raffles faced, and this is what scholars ever since have faced. Nevertheless, despite the obstacles, various answers – some still contentious – have been put forward. These are not answers of dry academia, but exciting responses to fascinating queries. What motivated Raffles must surely motivate us.

Tropical environments have traditionally been seen as less likely to contain anything that denotes 'ancient civilization'. Northern climes have jealously held on to that honour. Somehow the steamy jungle and wet rice paddies seemed less likely to have supported the intricacies of highly complex ancient cultures. Surely there was nothing south of the equator to compare with Greece, Rome and Egypt? But all too often history relies too heavily on the evidence of physical remains. Greece, Rome and Egypt impress because of their stone and concrete. Even the most beautiful wooden palace or monastery, however, would be unlikely to survive a millennium of monsoon and humidity. Nevertheless, in the absence of architectural evidence, how can one make claims for an ancient civilization? Raffles stands out because, even before the discovery of Borobudur, he was willing to entertain the possibility that Java did indeed play host to a great and ancient civilization.

Few of Raffles' colleagues in Southeast Asia shared this interest in history or his inclination to treat the Javanese and others as equals. Raffles believed, as did many eighteenth-century scholars, that there were three stages of human development – the Savage, the Barbarian and the Civilized. The anthropologist Nigel Barley, one of the experts on Raffles, believes that Raffles was also unusual in that he never thought that civilization necessarily had to have a white face. He held that it could have a brown face or a black face, and he clearly saw Java as having the potential for having been a civilization. Raffles' enormous and detailed *History of Java* can be seen as a claim for Java to be considered as 'civilized'. Raffles believed that there were various marks of each stage of human development, and that one of the marks of civilization was having the ability to create stone architecture. If a society was advanced enough to co-ordinate itself sufficiently well to be able to gather the raw materials, the labour force, the artistic skill and the energy to build, surely this was proof of its development. It would be proof of a classic antiquity, like the monuments of Greece and Rome in the West. If Raffles was to convince others of Java's status as a civilization, he had to show ancient temple ruins.

Even before Raffles arrived in Java, some evidence had been found, but the Dutch who ruled Java before the British were generally interested in trade, not history. Only on Raffles' arrival did the opportunity arise to rediscover a building of such magnitude, such skill, that no one could ever again doubt that, centuries ago, perhaps when Europe itself was in the depths of its Dark Ages, Java – indeed Southeast Asia – had been home to a great civilization. Raffles' discovery and restoration of the lost temple of Borobudur helped to prove that this was indeed the case.

JAVA

Java is a long island in the Malay Archipelago, extending for 650 miles more or less west to east. Lying at the juncture of the Asian and Australian continental plates, the island is one of the most volcanic on earth, with over 100 volcanoes of which an estimated 30 are active. Java has been the scene of many volcanic explosions, sometimes with terrible loss of life. As the island is effectively a string of volcanoes and volcanic plains it is relatively narrow – never more than 126 miles wide. The largest city today is Jakarta, which in Raffles' day was called Batavia.

Lying a little more than seven degrees south of the equator, the island experiences soaring temperatures and, being tropical, high levels of humidity. As a result of both high precipitation and the rich volcanic soils, the vegetation is extremely productive. Bamboo, palm, acacia, rubber, banana and teak are just some of the many trees. And, as Raffles discovered, the fauna are equally abundant – tiger, leopard, many species of bird, fish, snake and so on.

Although it is quite possible that man has lived on Java for a million years, the first locally produced written accounts date from the fifth century AD and were found near present-day Jakarta. It seems that at this time Java was a patchy series of kingdoms centred on dynasties dotted about the coastline and interior. A key element in the development of Javanese society and the maintenance of monarchical rule has been the ease with which rice has been cultivated. Such a regular and reliable crop has sustained population growth with few apparent difficulties. Rice-producing villages tended to subject themselves to local chiefs who, in turn, bowed before regional rulers.

We have some accounts of Java that date back many hundreds of years earlier. There is a reference to it in one version of the extended Indian epic *Ramayana*,

which may date back to the third century BC. In this version, reference is made to *Yavadvipa* ('Barley Island'). Here Java is described as being rich in gold and grain. It is suspected that, by this time, Indonesian merchants were already sailing to India and trading in woods and spices.

Another account comes from the late-first-century-AD Alexandrian geographer, Ptolemaeus. In his text there is mention of *Iabadiou* – a Greek translation of *Yavadvipa*. This may be evidence of the Roman Empire's first encounter with Java. Certainly there were Roman trading vessels in southern India that would have encountered any Indonesian sailors – and their goods would have made the long journey back to Italy and the provinces.

In subsequent centuries, trade throughout Southeast Asia massively increased and Java became an important trading stop for merchants. Travelling on board some of the ships were monks and teachers. As well, therefore, as an exchange of goods, there was an exchange of ideas. Initially such influences permeated merely the northern coasts of Java – the south is largely devoid of ports because of its geography – but we can assume that the centre of Java slowly began to change and mature too. So much so that, perhaps by the seventh century, the focus of civilization had moved to the centre of the island – around a string of twenty volcanoes. It was here that the evidence of a great civilization would one day be found.

In one of the most fertile areas on earth, these terraces have been carefully worked and reworked for over a thousand years.

Raffles

and

Java

'Mr Raffles ... was most courteous in his intercourse with all men. He always had a sweet expression towards Europeans as well as native gentlemen.

He was extremely affable and liberal, always commanding one's best attention.

He spoke in smiles ... It was plain to me that in all his sayings and doings there was the intelligence of a rising man, together with acuteness.

And if my experience be not at fault, there was not his superior in this world in skill or largeness of heart.'

CHAPTER

THOMAS STAMFORD RAFFLES

I was a strange wild fellow, insatiable in ambition, though meek as a maiden

C. E. WURTZBURG: *RAFFLES OF THE EASTERN ISLES*

Thomas Stamford Bingley Raffles was an untypical man of empire. He was no son of a duke, nor brother of an earl. He was born on his father's ship off Jamaica on 6 July 1781.

'It is singularly appropriate,' wrote his biographer Wurtzburg, 'that Raffles should have been born at sea and that one who would later rank among our empire-builders should have survived the perils of the West Indies to live and build in the East Indies.'

Raffles' father, Captain Benjamin Raffles, was the master of the ship *Ann* that at that time was involved in trading throughout the Caribbean. Little is known of Captain Raffles except that he was a Yorkshireman married to a woman called Anne. Thomas was their second son, the first having died in infancy. Equally little is known of the young Raffles once he had been christened on their return to England at the parish church of Eaton Bishop in Herefordshire. He was given the name Stamford Bingley apparently out of respect for his two godfathers, Mr Stamford and Mr Bingley.

Captain Raffles appears to have been a senior figure in the West Indian trade and yet financially unsuccessful. With another five children following Thomas (one, a son, died), pressure built increasingly on the family finances. As a result it seems that Thomas's upbringing was not a comfortable one and, at the age of fourteen, after only two years of schooling in Hammersmith, west of London, the impoverishment of his family led to him being taken from school. He would later lament: 'The deficiency of my early education has never been fully supplied.'

In 1795, the fourteen year old began work, joining a company that he would spend his entire working life with – the East India Company. The Company was

6 July 1781 – born on board father's ship off Jamaica

1795 – joined East India Company

April 1805 – sailed to Penang

1810 – met Lord Minto

May 1811 – helped launch invasion of Java

18 September 1811 – Dutch and French capitulate in Java

November/December 1811 – first trip to Yogyakarta

June 1812 – defeated Sultan of Yogyakarta

November/December 1813 – trip to Yogyakarta
and tour of east Java

26 April 1815 – set off to tour island

18 May 1815 – first saw Borobudur

January 1816 – set off to tour island

18 January 1816 – hears of dimissal from post
of Lieutenant-Governor

24 March 1816 – left Java

1817 – published History of Java.
Knighted by Prince Regent

1818 – appointed to Benkulu

1819 – founded Singapore

1824 – returned to London.
Founded London Zoological Society.
Mother died

6 July 1826 – died of brain haemorrhage.

Britain's front line in the East. Though essentially a private trading company, it was supervised by the government during its expansion into new and financially beneficial markets. Ruled by a Governor-General in Calcutta, the Company's area of influence focused specifically on India but extended beyond the subcontinent and throughout Asia for thousands of miles.

THE EAST INDIA COMPANY AND SOUTHEAST ASIA

Until the end of the sixteenth century, the Portuguese supplied the English markets with pepper and spices, but prices were rising. The London-based East India Company was subsequently formed in 1600, by merchants keen to deal directly with traders in Asia, rather than through the middlemen of the Mediterranean – initially the Portugese and more recently the Dutch.

From the sixteenth century, the European naval powers of Spain, Holland, Britain and particularly Portugal had been extending their frontiers in Asia. The passage to the Americas, the West and East Indies, and China fuelled an enormous expansion in trade. In the late sixteenth century the Dutch set sail for the East Indies, keen to trade in spices and other luxury goods. Such trade was riven with dangers, and force was increasingly used to secure advantage. But the profits were motivation enough to undergo the trials and tribulations of such long sea voyages.

Sir Thomas Stamford Raffles was a precocious young man of 30 when he became Lieutenant-Governor of Java. He had a voracious appetite for knowledge leading to his rediscovery of Borobudur.

The Dutch East India Company (VOC) had been founded in 1602, some years after the first visit of a Dutch ship to Asia. The Netherlands joined in the battle with Portugal and Britain for the lucrative trade. Much of the trade, however, consisted of shipments not to and from Europe but between the thousands of islands of insular Southeast Asia and mainland Asia, and it was known as the 'country' trade. Silks, cotton, tea and coffee were particularly successful. A ragbag of tawdry ships carried such wares in the quest for easy money. Little interest was shown in the Asians themselves.

Britain at this time was a star that had yet to shine. Its interest tended to focus west on the Americas but a growing market to the East was beginning to stir colonial ambitions. By the mid 1700s Britain was under assault in both Europe and the Americas. Isolated by slow and inconsistent communications over thousands of miles, the affairs of the Indian subcontinent and Southern Asia developed at their own pace and were often little affected by events at home. The three trading corporations – the East India Company, the French Compagnie des Indes and the

27

Maritime trade has been the lifeblood of Southeast Asia for 2000 years. In Raffles' period, the British, Dutch, French and Portuguese vied for supremacy in the purchase and distribution of the area's many valuable commodities.

Dutch VOC – often without the approval and sometimes even the knowledge of their governments, variously competed and fought with one another. Fleets protected their interests and local armies were trained to do the same. The early history of the British East India Company was marked by failure. The Dutch, in particular, resisted firmly any attempts to shift them from their territories. Indeed so entrenched did the Dutch appear that the British more or less accepted their supremacy in the Malay Archipelago.

In the mid eighteenth century Robert Clive led a small British army to victory over the French and extended British control over an increased area of India. This defeat of the French in India made the East India Company an Asian as well as an Indian company. The trading routes to China were now safely open and officials back in London delighted in the increasing profits. (For the employees of the Company, life was less joyful. Six or seven out of every ten men sent to the East died there.)

During the eighteenth century the Dutch too expanded their sphere of power, both by direct force and by striking alliances with local rulers. Having imposed themselves, they often introduced trading monopolies to ensure sole control of the produce of the islands. They restricted the cultivation of the fine spices, cloves and nutmeg to the islands of eastern Indonesia. Elsewhere spice trees were deliberately destroyed to protect such monopolies. A little later they established plantations, and introduced crops such as coffee into Java. Sometimes, particularly in Java, relying on the local aristocracy to support them, the Dutch pushed things so far that local powers collapsed and the Dutch were left effectively in full control. But corruption and general poor financial management led the Dutch East India Company into bankruptcy by the end of the eighteenth century, and the Netherlands state assumed responsibility for its debts and territories.

As the century reached its close, Raffles was working as a clerk at East India House, the central London offices of the Company in Leadenhall Street. In this large, fobidding building, Thomas worked in the Secretary's office – one of maybe 50 or 60 clerks. The writer Charles Lamb, who had entered the same office three years earlier, described the regime: 'I am cruelly engaged; on Friday I was at the office from ten in the morning (two hours dinner excepting) to eleven at night . . . I do not keep a Holy Day now once in ten times . . . confusion blast all mercantile transactions . . . . In this mournful weather I sit moping where I now write, jammed in between four walls and writing by candlelight most melancholy.'

The pay was low, the work monotonous; but Raffles was determined to succeed,

The East India Company Headquarters at Leadenhall Street, London. The building no longer exists but was once home to a vital part of Britain's expanding empire. For a humble clerk like Raffles, it was an arduous, even miserable place.

and after work he studied at home. He later remembered the pain of being told by his mother that they could not afford the candles he was using to read.

At the age of 24, after ten years of dedication and toil, he finally received the news he had been so earnestly working towards. He was promoted – and what a promotion it was. From a £70-a-year clerk to £1500-a-year Assistant Secretary to the Government of Prince of Wales Island (Penang) in Malaya.

In April 1805, before departing, he married Olivia Fancourt in Bloomsbury, London. Olivia was a lively woman who had been married before; rumours circulated that she had been the mistress of the Secretary of the East India Company and that Raffles' lofty promotion was by way of a bribe for them to keep quiet. Raffles denied this: 'My wife was in no manner connected with him; they never saw each other, neither could my advancement in life possibly be accelerated by marriage. It gave me no connexions, no wealth but on the contrary a load of debt which I had to clear off. It increased my difficulties and thus increased my energies. It gave me domestic enjoyment and thus contributed to my happiness; but in no way can my advancement in life be accounted owing to that connexion.'

For one reason or another, Raffles was dogged by rumour and accusation throughout his life. The reason, above all, seemed to be that his promotions and positions came to him at such a young age – causing jealously and spite among older colleagues.

Such promotions, however, were well earned. On the six-month voyage to Penang he taught himself Malay, a skill which few of his peers seemed to understand would be useful. Penang had become British only in 1786 and had been virtually uninhabited at the time. However, this little island, just fifteen miles long and ten miles wide, was seen as having the potential to be an important staging post. Raffles now found himself in a completely alien and exciting world, and his first impression was one of wonder. A fellow traveller wrote:

The Island presented a most beautiful and irregular outline, involved in those delicate tints of grey which, as the sun rose, through a humid atmosphere, changed to a beautiful pink . . . As we approached, the deepening tints became more and more vivid, point after point opening gradually to our view, until the whole extent of the picturesque Isle formed one side of our splendid panorama . . . The town spreads itself naturally over a little point of land jutting out into the sea, which seemed so expressly formed for its Establishment that one can scarcely believe that it was with such infinite labour and expense that the East India Company succeeded in making the space habitable by clearing away the thick jungle which formerly covered it.

Once landed, Raffles soon discovered that the British administration was highly inefficient. This, however, served to provide him with every opportunity to make a name for himself by doing his utmost to put things right. His enormous energy and attention to detail soon paid off – long complex letters penned by him began to be noticed by his superiors '. . . with respect to timber, there is considerable supply . . .' '. . . with respect of the principal points of commercial advantage . . .' '. . . I am inclined to think that nearly the whole of the pepper, the produce of the Island, is fit for the Europe market . . .'

A colleague, Captain Thomas Travers, was impressed with the young man's abilities:

Being of a cheerful lively disposition and very fond of Society it was surprising how he was able to entertain so hospitably as he did and yet labour so much as he was known to do at the time, not only in his official capacity but in acquiring a general knowledge of the history, Government and local interests of the neighbouring States; and this he was greatly aided in doing by conversing freely with the natives.

The public dispatches were also entrusted to him and, in fact, he had the entire weight and trouble attendant on the formation of a new Government. . . . Few men, but those who were immediately on the spot at the time, can form any idea of the difficult task which he had to perform . . . he gave most general satisfaction . . .

So effective was he in these tasks that he began to consider how to ascend even further up the corporation hierarchy. Slowly over a period of five years, he gained respect and acknowledgement. There was time for leisure too – for dancing, theatricals, reading and riding. But life carried its risks: there was, apart from riding, no outdoor exercise – not even tennis or cricket – while excessive eating and drinking, as well as poor choice of clothing and local fevers, made it a tough post to survive. The 'weak maiden' Raffles suffered as much as anyone: 'My constitution was always delicate; with care I have no doubt it could last as long here as in England. Without it, it will soon break up. I am afraid they will work the willing horse to death; all I ask is to see an end to it . . .'

He decided to seek a new post. To effect this, he chose to make himself known to the Governor-General of India, who was at that time Gilbert Elliot, the Earl of Minto. In 1810 the 29 year old expressly travelled to Calcutta where he managed to meet the Governor-General himself. Fortunately for Raf-

Raffles was extremely fortunate to find a sponsor like Lord Minto (above). Minto had the ability to recognize the talents and energies of Raffles and put them to good use. Both men believed that the colonisers should help the colonised.

fles, Lord Minto was one of the few to realize how important it was in the governing of foreign races for the governors to speak the languages of the governed. 'How much prejudice to the interest of the Company, how much vexation, extortion and credulity towards our Native Subjects, how much individual shame and ruin have resulted from the cause [of ignorance of foreign languages].' He too was impressed with the young Raffles.

Raffles had heard that a post was available in the islands of the Moluccas, but was unsuccessful in his attempts to secure it. Instead Raffles, with his thorough knowledge of the region, was encouraged to keep Minto informed of the advantages of taking the Dutch-controlled island of Java.

'. . . On the mention of Java,' wrote Raffles later, 'his lordship cast a look of such scrutiny, anticipation and kindness upon me, as I shall never forget. "Yes," said he, "I shall be happy to receive any information you can give me." From this moment all my plans were devoted to create such an interest regarding Java as should lead to its annexation to our Eastern Empire . . .'

AT WAR WITH NAPOLEON

A European island of great value was Corsica in the Mediterranean and its possession had changed hands many times. It had only been French for a year when Napoleon Bonaparte was born there on 15 August 1769.

By the time Napoleon entered the military academy in Paris in 1784, France was undergoing radical change. The Bourbon monarchy and the old regime were in the process of being swept away. Great change brought great opportunity, and Napoleon's career soon took off. Placed in charge of a demoralized Army of Italy, he launched a brilliant series of campaigns that caused Austria, the rulers of Italy, to sue for peace. Napoleon's next command was to prepare for an invasion of England, but he concluded that this was impossible until France ruled the waves. It would be much more intelligent to hit Britain where it would hurt most – in her trade. If he could control Turkish-ruled Egypt, he could cut the route to India. The economic effects on Britain would force them, he was sure, to make peace.

The French government was happy to approve the plan and he was given 40,000 troops. The difficulty was getting them past the British Royal Navy to Egypt. This he succeeded in achieving and he won two battles against the Turks – one at Alexandria, the other at the Pyramids. However, when the British Admiral Sir Horatio Nelson destroyed his fleet anchored at Aboukir Bay in August 1798, Napoleon's mobility was destroyed, and his lines of supply were cut. Napoleon abandoned his soldiers and hurried back to France.

These actions made it very clear that France was implacably opposed to both Britain and her trade successes. But war was exhausting them both, and in 1802 they signed a fragile peace treaty. The truce did not last long, and war broke out again in May 1803. Britain feared invasion until Nelson and his fleet put paid to that idea at Trafalgar on 21 October 1805. So Napoleon turned east and in a remarkable campaign took his Grand Army of 500,000 men to Austerlitz, where he defeated the Prussians and Austrians. Only a year later Prussia declared war afresh on France but was defeated again at Jena and Auerstadt. So Napoleon felt ready to turn on Britain one more time. This time he imposed a continental blockade in an effort to destroy the British economy. Portugal refused to comply and Napoleon declared war in 1807. The Peninsular War in Portugal and then Spain was to last seven years. Meanwhile Napoleon once again fought and beat the Prussians, Russians and Austrians. By 1810 his empire was at the furthest extent. And that, since 1795, had included the Netherlands – and therefore all of the Netherlands' colonies.

Britain – who had been more or less allies of the Dutch – could not allow the French flag to fly for too long in Southeast Asia. That, it was felt, would jeopardize not only her own trading position there but also her prized and essential control of India. This gave Raffles the chance he wanted to justify the conquest of Java.

By 1810, therefore, when Raffles saw Minto in Calcutta, the British authorities in India were already wondering how to reduce French influence in Java and other islands. For this reason, Minto was receptive to Raffles' petition, in which he wrote: 'The resources of Java are extensive. It is the rice granary of the East. If the Island was freed from restriction, it could more than cover its expenditure. Coffee, pepper, cotton, tobacco and indigo, etc., can be cultivated with such success that every other Settlement in that quarter of the globe could be undersold. Its timber resources alone would render its possession an object of the greatest importance . . .'

Minto was impressed with this young administrator and, having already assigned the post in the Moluccas to someone else, appointed Raffles as his Agent in Malacca, Malaya, to collect information to assist a British invasion of the island. Here Raffles began to employ a Malay scribe and later teacher, Munshi Abdullah. Abdullah described Raffles thus:

When I first saw Mr Raffles, he struck me as being of middle stature, neither too short nor too tall. His brow was broad, the sign of large heartedness; his head betokened his good understanding; his hair being fair betokened courage; his ears being large betokened quick hearing; his eyebrows were thick, and his left eye squinted a little; his nose was high; his cheeks a little hollow; his lips narrow, the sign of oratory and persuasiveness; his mouth was wide; his neck was long, and the colour of his body was not purely white; his breast was well-formed; his waist slender; his legs to proportion and he walked with a stoop . . . .

Now, I observed his habit was to be always in deep thought. He was most courteous in his intercourse with all men. He always had a sweet expression towards Europeans as well as native gentlemen. He was extremely affable and liberal, always commanding one's best attention. He spoke in smiles.

Now, Mr Raffles took great interest in looking into the origin of nations, and their manners and customs of olden times, examining what would elucidate the same. He was especially quick in the uptake of Malay with its variations. He delighted to use the proper idioms as the natives do; he was active in studying words and their place in phrases and not until we had told him would he state that the English had another mode.

I also perceived that he hated the habit of the Dutch who lived in Malacca of running down the Malays and they detested him in return; so much so that they would not sit down beside him. But Mr Raffles loved always to be on good terms with the Malays, the poorest could speak to him; and while all the great folk in Malacca came to wait on him daily, whether Malays or Europeans, yet they could not find out his object in coming there – his ulterior intentions. But it was plain to me that in all his sayings and doings there was the intelligence of a rising man, together with acuteness. And if my experience be not at fault, there was not his superior in this world in skill or largeness of heart.

THE INVASION OF JAVA

In May 1811, Minto and Raffles left Malacca and headed for Java, accompanying a fleet of transports carrying 11,000 soldiers (3000 Europeans, the rest Sepoys). They tacked for seven weeks against the monsoon winds, before arriving off the Javanese coast near Batavia. From his ship, Raffles sent a note to the Dutch, in which he argued:

England has in every period, sometimes in concert with other powers, sometimes single and alone, been the champion and defender of Europe, the hope of those whose fate was not yet consummated, the refuge and consolation of the fallen – for France has been with equal uniformity the common enemy of all nations. Between these two the option must be made and on that question the extinction of their metropolis has left the Colonies of Holland to their own free judgement. Their country has expired.

The Dutch chose to fight. However, the forces on Java, while outnumbering the British, were of inferior quality, consisting of a few French – some there for desertion or other crimes – a sullen Dutch contingent and a poorly trained native detachment. The fighting that ensued between the two forces was patchy but at times bloody. It took over a month for the British to quell the resistance and be in a position to declare Java 'taken'.

The East India Company were happy to see the French removed but amazed that Minto, ignoring instructions that they were to take Java then leave it to the inhabitants, had decided to stay on. Wasting no time, Minto began the work of reorganizing the government and issuing a declaration of intent. He also announced his choice as the new Lieutenant-Governor of 'Java and its dependencies': 'His Excellency has been pleased to appoint the Honourable Thomas Raffles, Lieutenant-Governor of Java . . . [he] will exercise the powers of Government, and will be invested with all the authorities appertaining thereto in the fullest and amplest manner.'

There were those who felt aggrieved at this appointment, but as Minto himself explained, he had given the post to the man who had done most to earn it. Raffles' enormously detailed preparations for the invasion had been invaluable (not least for gaining the support of most Malay princes), and Minto saw in him a man who earnestly intended to do his utmost for the people of Java as well as for the East India Company. At their last dinner together Minto declared: 'While we are here, let us do all the good we can.'

'I am here alone,' wrote Raffles, soon afterwards, 'without any advice in a new country with a large native population of not less than six or seven million . . , a great proportion of foreign Europeans and a standing army of not less than 7000 men . . . [But] if a man [is] fully and seriously determined on accomplishing any undertaking within human power at all, he [will] succeed by diligence and attention.'

Batavia was first settled by the Dutch in 1619. It was intended to be their main trading centre in Southeast Asia. A few Dutch buildings still remain in the sprawl of modern Jakarta.

DISCOVERING THE TEMPLE

LIFE IN BOGOR

As Lieutenant-Governor, Raffles moved into the Governor's residence at Bogor, about four hours south of Batavia. Raffles described the view as: 'most delightfully picturesque. The descent from the house almost precipitate – in the bottom a valley filled with rice . . . in the background a magnificent range of mountains, wooded to the top and capped in clouds . . . nothing can exceed the beauty of the scene.'

His ADC, Captain Thomas Travers, who had been with him in Penang, later wrote: 'the house was constantly filled with visitors . . . we had a large party at breakfast, dinner and supper, from which he never absented himself, but, on the contrary, was always one of the most animated at table, and yet contrived to find sufficient time to write [official business] . . . .'

At the residence, Raffles and Olivia entertained frequently. He was always willing to discuss matters of policy, science or nature with anyone who enquired. The local *Java Government Gazette* carried the following report of one of his entertainments:

> *On Sunday last, the Lieutenant-Governor gave a dejeuner and fishing party [for Javanese guests] . . . at a romantic spot situated on the banks of great river. A spacious temporary building had been constructed for the occasion. Breakfast was announced, which was laid out with taste, and the Governor's band played several popular tunes . . . a few minutes after the company was seated [by] the river some intoxicating vegetable was thrown in by which the fish became immediately inebriated . . . and easy prey . . . . After enjoying the sport for about an hour, the party returned highly delighted . . . .*

Card games, music and dance filled many an evening – though his work never suffered. He would work after the party if need be. Raffles' biographer, C.E. Wurtzburg, paints a picture of the aid Olivia gave him in these duties: 'He was admirably supported by the lovely Olivia. She had been at first rather shocked by the native dress that even leading Dutch ladies affected. The crude mass of jewellery, too, and above all the betel-chewing offended her sense of taste. Naturally her implied criticism of well-established customs was at first resented; that a foreigner should regard herself as superior in manners was not easily borne. But her personal charm, her sweet, gentle and sincere nature, soon prevailed.'

Among those entertained by Raffles were the officials of the previous Dutch administration. He needed them to stay on, as there were too few Britons to run Java without them. 'The late Council came forward in a body and after taking the Oath before me I am sorry to add got most jovially tipsy at my house. . .'

Having established a working relationship with the Dutch, Raffles turned to establishing good relations with the native sultans. For Raffles, Java meant more than trade. But to achieve anything he would have to gain local support. He was eager to convince them he had their best interests at heart in his efforts to reduce piracy, disease, and the trade in slaves – all of which had been tolerated, even exploited, by the Dutch: 'It is the duty of a colonial government to serve the interests of the inhabitants and not the interests of the mother country.'

Later in his life Raffles was to write: 'Let Britain not be remembered as the tempest whose course was desolation, but as the gate of Spring, reviving the slumbering seeds of mind, and calling them to life from the winter of ignorance and oppression.'

The government at home could at any time declare Java a King's Colony, and appoint a soldier to govern it, as was common practice. Raffles therefore had to work in the knowledge that at a moment's notice he might be replaced with a military officer. But he also knew that it might never happen, and that the quicker he worked, securing as many successes as possible, the better his chances were of being allowed to remain as Lieutenant-Governor.

His notion that the only justification of Empire is the wellbeing of the inhabitants was not really a policy that the East India Company wanted to hear about, let alone to implement. Minto's own son, Gilbert Elliot, disliked Raffles, of whom he wrote: 'Raffles was neither born nor bred a gentleman – and we all know that the nicer habits and feelings of a gentleman are not to be acquired . . . Raffles was a very able man with his pen, and well understood the habits and peculiarities of the Eastern peoples. But he was unfit to govern.'

Such criticism was harsh. Raffles felt that Java's produce, including rice and

The fine Governor's house – built by the Dutch – was much enjoyed by Raffles. There he could work tirelessly, surrounded by the natural environment he loved so much.

pepper could earn sufficient income to keep his employers happy and allow him to embrace the task of reform. He immediately saw that the previous Dutch administration had been harsh and counter-productive. Corruption, injustice and *ad hoc* taxation were widespread. Raffles decided to divide Java into sixteen areas, each with a Resident, who acted for the government. A land revenue system was introduced, based on the idea that all land was now to be considered the property of the government, with a land tax paid direct to the government. He also curtailed the powers of the local ruling élites. These major reforms involved a great deal of upheaval and man-hours. They also necessitated the launching of a full survey of Java's land. The survey was never completed, but one of the side-effects was that, for the first time, representatives of the government were sent out to find out more about Java, its land, its people and, as a result, its history.

Raffles' determination to improve the situation of the Javanese can be seen as a paternal benevolence. While he was willing to allow for the likelihood of Java having once played host to an ancient civilization, he was dismayed at the cultural state of Javanese society before him. In a letter to William Marsden, author of *The History of Sumatra*, he wrote: '[They] are a people by no means far advanced in civilisation . . . Their generally wandering and predatory life induces them to follow the fortune of a favourite Chief, and to form themselves into a variety of separate clans. They may not be ineptly compared, as far as their habits and notions go, to some of the borderers in North Britain, not many centuries ago.'

Nor should it be forgotten that Raffles, when necessary, could be tough. For example, the Sultan of Yogyakarta was showing resistance to British authority. Raffles hoped to avoid a conflict, but relations between his Representative Crawfurd and the Sultan were deteriorating. On 28 November 1811, Raffles himself went to try to resolve matters peacefully. Showing great courage, he managed to secure a treaty. However, it was not to last – the following year, a conflict broke out.

I should mention that the Craton was a regular fortified position about three miles in circumference, surrounded by a wide and deep ditch, with a wall 45 feet high, defended by well-constructed bastions, and ramparts . . . at the period of assault it was calculated there could not be less than 11,000 men within, while large parties of up to 4000 occupied positions without, blocking up the main roads . . .

. . . The Sultan refusing to comply with my [demand for unconditional surrender] we commenced a heavy cannonade . . . it was immediately returned . . . [Then] an assault was made . . . ; we soon got possession of the ramparts, and turned their guns upon them . . . the fighting was violent and bloody [but] in less than three hours it was over . . .

Even though life was lost in this assault, Raffles believed it was for the general good. His desire to improve living conditions motivated him to press on with introducing vaccinations, reducing the flow of opium and improving health care, He also prohibited, from the beginning of 1813, the importation of slaves into Java. 'It is repugnant to every principle of enlightened administration.'

Communications to and from Britain were tortuously slow. But one piece of bad news that arrived towards the start of 1815 was that Napoleon had been captured and Britain had agreed to return Java to the Netherlands. This was dispiriting news, for which Raffles really had little response until, a few weeks later, he heard that Napoleon had escaped from Elba and war had broken out again. Raffles was overjoyed, as it meant that Java would remain British for at least a while longer. He continued his work – and his explorations.

THE DESIRE FOR KNOWLEDGE

In his residence at Bogor, Raffles worked tirelessly. His predecessors, the men of the Dutch East Indies, had shown little interest in the history of Java. Although a few had established the Batavian Society of Arts and Sciences, of which Raffles would become president, they were for the most part merchants who sought cash not culture. This lack of interest was not specific to the Dutch; few Europeans at this time cared for the past or what they could learn from it. Raffles knew therefore that some of his own peers thought Java – indeed Southeast Asia as a whole – was a barbaric place with, effectively, no history of note. He was determined to prove them wrong, and although his workload as Governor was already enormous, he decided to write a vast 'History of Java'. As Raffles' biographer, C.E.Wurtzburg, wrote:

Apart from the importance that such a book would and indeed did achieve, the task of collecting and preparing the material made it essential that no aspect should be omitted. This stimulated enquiries and investigation in the widest possible field. This again suited Raffles' catholic taste. It is, in fact, difficult to determine which branch of science lay closest to his heart; whichever one forms the subject of a letter, that one seems to be his particular interest. Although his enthusiasm was all-embracing, he cannot be regarded as a mere dilettante, turning at random, as fancy prompted, from one subject to another. One of his special claims to recognition as a scientist is that he was an exact and systematic observer and, in this respect, ahead of his time. He applied to science the same meticulous care, the same search for facts, the same patient industry as distinguished his administration. Unlimited curiosity and insistence on actual data mark the scientist. These were the characteristics of Raffles.

Raffles' home must have been a jumble of flora and numerous other artefacts brought to him by his employees or the Javanese themselves. When Raffles left Java, he took with him masses of material, some of which was tragically lost during a fire on a later voyage.

Although Raffles was certainly critical of the behaviour of some of the Javanese that he encountered, he had a
great respect for their culture and commissioned some fine portraits of them for his book.

Raffles began accumulating specimens and information – anything that would
be of use. His habit, throughout his life, remained the same. We know from
accounts of Raffles' postings elsewhere that he would employ locals to carry out
searches and explorations for him. No doubt he did the same while in Java. His
Malay teacher Munshi Abdullah recorded such events in Malacca:

> He kept four persons on wages, each in their peculiar departments; one to go to the forests
> in search of various kinds of leaves, flowers, fungi and such like. Another he sent to collect
> all kinds of flies, grasshoppers, bees, scorpions . . . Another he sent to seek for coral, shells,
> oysters, cockles . . . and another to collect animals . . .
>   . . . in the evenings, after tea, he would take ink, pen and paper, after the candles had
> been lighted, reclining with closed eyes in a manner that I often took to be sleep; but in an
> instant he would be up and write for a while till he went to recline again. The next morning
> he would go to what he had written and read it while walking backwards and forwards,
> when, out of ten sheets, probably he would only give three or four to his copying clerk to
> enter into the books, and the others he would tear up. Such was his daily habit . . .
>   Mr Raffles [also] took great interest in looking into the origin of nations, and their

manners and customs of olden times . . . his habit was to be always in deep thought . . .
He was an earnest enquirer into past history and gave up nothing till he had probed
it to the bottom.

This interest manifested itself very clearly at Raffles' appearances as president of the Batavian Society of Arts and Sciences. The first meeting was held on 23 April 1813 and he sketched out what he thought should be his objectives. In essence, he sought to investigate the 'East'. He hoped that the enthusiasm and enquiry of men like Colonel Mackenzie, Captain Baker and a young Dutch officer named H.C. Cornelius would take them into previously little explored parts of the island.

Since French rule, more and more temples and stone insciptions had been discovered on the island. However, it required a man of Raffles' insight to fit the pieces of the puzzle together and realize that some time in the distant past there had once been a great civilization on Java. Raffles was unusual for his time in that not only was he able to conceive of such a thing, he was willing to believe it.

FIRST REPORTS

Hitherto, these important monuments of antiquity have excited but
little interest in the European rulers of the land; inscriptions that would have enlightened
history have been allowed to remain in obscurity; and structures that defy the imitation of
modern art, to moulder into premature decay.   COLONEL THOMAS WATSON, 1816

The Dutch, having been largely concerned with trade, had placed restrictions on travel to central Java. There had been a number of learned men among the Dutch élite who had looked into Java's past but, overall, exploration had figured very low in their priorities, and the south and centre of Java had been infrequently visited. The French lifted the restrictions and, under the terms of the peace treaty with the Sultan of Yogyakarta, a large area of central Java in particular was open to investigation. It was in this area that Borobudur would be discovered. The Dutch did know, however, about the extensive ruins at the Hindu complex of Prambanan, possibly because they lay alongside the main road south to Yogyakarta. When they travelled down to visit the Sultan they would have seen the piles of rocks and stones – and indeed some drawings were made of Prambanan in the early 1800s. But there was no reason to go towards the location of Borobudur – there was no court in this region and it wasn't on the way to anywhere else. Even at the height of their power, there were only a few hundred Dutch in Java at any one time, and the further one travelled out of Batavia the less receptive the Javanese were to foreign authority. Few Dutch therefore had the time or inclination even to consider going off to explore.

The Dutch – and later Raffles – commissioned illustrations of ruins in central Java. These alone persuaded Raffles that an ancient civilization had existed, but the scale and craftsmanship of Borobudur was final proof.

There are Javanese reports from the time that refer to the hill of statues and the place on which there were these images of 'warriors in cages' and so on. But even if the Dutch had passed by, unless they had actually climbed up the hill and taken the trouble to inspect it at first hand they might not have realized that a man-made structure lay underfoot.

Raffles' inquisitive mind, on the other hand, rarely rested, and he actively encouraged travellers to cover the island and send him their accounts. One such report arrived from a Colonel Colin Mackenzie after a journey to central Java. Mackenzie had spent over a decade in India, where he was Surveyor General of Madras, and was surprised, when he visited Prambanan, to see familiar gods in a remote island that was largely Muslim. He later wrote this account of his first sight of the ruins:

January 19,1812: Arrived at Brambana [Prambanan] at 9 a.m. by very deep bad roads, and put up at the Chinaman's Bandaree near the road. While breakfast was getting ready I stept out, walked across and along the road; and by a path winding near the river, wandered among ruins evidently belonging to some great building, till at last I got into the square, enclosing the Ancient Pyramidal Mounds of stone . . . The whole of this Pile, Pyramid, or Mass of Stone may be perhaps about 60 feet high, and to the doors which I entered about 25 feet . . . After some refreshment . . . proceeded . . . to perambulate the ruins; chairs were provided, covered with canopies of leaves and each carried by four men on poles of bamboo, but my impatience did not always permit me to avail myself of this convenient coverture from the sun's scorching rays, amidst the tantalizing ruins that surrounded us . . . The bushes here are so thick that we did not perceive till we came

suddenly on them two gigantic figures of porters apparently kneeling on pedestals facing each other, resting on clubs held in one hand . . .

We were lodged in the Chinaman's house – a sleeping room and tolerable beds were allotted to each on either side of a hall, where the family eat their own meals . . . The evening was passed after dinner in writing our notes . . .

The interior structure of the masonry is disclosed, and shews that no cement whatever was used, the stones having been cut and fitted to each other, probably in a quarry . . .

The size of the trees that have overgrown these Temples are sufficient indications of a great age . . . we were literally obliged to cut our way; the path winded back and brought us in the hollow over several blocks of cut stone, the ruins of dilapidated walls . . . the site is entirely overgrown with bushes and luxuriant verdure, grass and trees; it was in vain to go further; the rain increased; it was getting late . . . a huge trunk impeded further progress . . .

This . . . corroborates the tradition of a City being here founded by a Foreign Colony, whose Artists being ingenious, chose a spot near to the best materials . . . we might suspect that in the same Government, Empire and People, these marks of refined superior skill . . . originated . . .

Raffles was intrigued by such reports and sought more such detail as he recalled in his *History of Java*: 'Considering it a matter of importance, that a more extensive and detailed survey should be made . . . I availed myself of the services of Captain George Baker to survey, measure and take draughts of all the buildings, images, and inscriptions which this magnificent mass of ruins presented.'

Captain Baker was as impressed as Colonel Mackenzie: 'Nothing can exceed the air of melancholy, desolation, and ruin, which this spot presents . . . The patronage and encouragement which the arts and sciences must have received, and the inexhaustible wealth and resources which the Javanese of those times must have possessed!'

Raffles was increasingly excited by what was being reported to him: 'In few countries with which we are yet acquainted are more extensive ruins to be found of temples dedicated to an ancient worship . . . The whole energies and resources of the country would appear to have been applied to the construction of these noble edifices . . .'

No one realized that the jungle still concealed the noblest edifice of all.

CORNELIUS

On arrival in Java, Raffles, with relatively few officials of his own on whom he could call, had to encourage the Dutch officials to remain in their place. Most were happy to do so, as they had nowhere else to go. It was an odd relationship but it was the French that Britain disliked – indeed the Dutch government had fled to Britain when Napoleon had invaded. Both countries assumed that once the war with Napoleon was over, the island would probably be returned to Holland. Raffles himself hoped it would never come to that.

Every two or three weeks Raffles, when not on tour of the island, left Government House at Bogor, visited Batavia and held open house. On these occasions anyone could come to him with their problems or requests. He tried hard to maintain good relations with both the Javanese and the Dutch. Many would come and listen to the traditional music of the gamelan and then eat with him. In Nigel Barley's view, Raffles cultivated good relationships with traditional rulers and convinced them that the way to impress him was not to send him slave children, but ancient documents and historical works. All got to learn that the way to Raffles' heart was to bring him something of an archaeological or a cultural nature. The likelihood is that this is how he first learned of Borobudur.

The exact date when Raffles first heard of a massive building obscured by jungle is uncertain, but it was probably in 1814, for it was then that Raffles chose to spend some of his scarce resources on commissioning the Dutch officer H.C. Cornelius to investigate. Cornelius was an engineer who had worked alongside Mackenzie and made beautiful drawings of Prambanan. Cornelius, who had probably imagined that Prambanan was the best Java had to offer, was eager to accept Raffles' charge, head southwest and see whether the new reports would uncover something even more remarkable. Journeying through Java was not easy, but what Cornelius saw at the end of the journey soon made him forget the hardships endured. The Javanese took him to the 'Hill of Statues'. The archaeologist John Miksic gives us an impression of Cornelius's arrival at the hill:

I imagine what Cornelius first saw when he came to this site would have been an area covered with secondary scrub, which is actually quite a lot thicker than normal primary forest. Here and there he might have seen a statue or two, sticking out of the ground. I imagine that's what first drew his attention as he began to explore the site. Only gradually, I think, would he have begun to realize that there was something much bigger than just a few statues on a natural hill. You sometimes have to explore an area for a long time before what seem to be just natural features, accidental juxtapositions of stones, suddenly begin to seem unnatural, man-made. Obviously he was not told that the whole hill was in fact a man-made monument, it only began to appear to him that way after he had explored in the undergrowth for some time. I've had one or two experiences like this also, not on the scale

of Borobudur but seeing what turns out to be some kind of old temple for the very first time. And it takes a while before it dawns on you – it's not like a great shout of 'Eureka! I have discovered a new building.' It takes a while, because you're scrambling through bushes and overgrowth and just trying to get a picture of what's there, and then a kind of a hypothesis begins to form in your mind and it gradually grows on you after a while. I assume that that's what Cornelius felt also.

Cornelius had no official training, and none of the many other monuments in the area had yet been restored. So all he had seen were piles of stones, jumbled-up remains; maybe the relief or head off a lower section here and there, but certainly no previous experience that would have prepared him for seeing an entire man-made hill. He would probably have been expecting to see a few statues on a hill, and it was a great act of deduction that through the dense undergrowth he gradually began to pick out the form of something extraordinary. Slowly he must have picked up that there were alignments of stones, and he probably followed these along, realizing that they were very large, continuous, connected walls.

Cornelius would have seen the occasional statue lying in the dirt but it needed a real leap of imagination to guess that the hill on which he was walking was, in fact, a temple.

Excited by the discovery, Cornelius gradually began to see through the foliage and put together a mental picture of what lay before – and beneath – him. He began to make drawings (of which nearly 40 survive), and sent some of these with his report to Raffles.

RAFFLES SEES THE TEMPLE

Raffles' days were full of reports coming and going – he was renowned for sending and receiving multiple petitions, letters and documents day after day. Then, one day in 1814, a document was delivered by messenger that contained something special – Cornelius's report. Needless to say, Raffles, who was at heart a natural scientist, was extremely excited at this new find and determined to see the ruins at the earliest opportunity. His first duties, however, lay in the governing of Java and its dependencies. With only his slim civil service and always the pressures of financial constraint, it was difficult for him simply to leave someone else in control for a while and spend the necessary few weeks travelling south to the waiting Cornelius. His workload was simply too great – and, in truth, it was not going at all smoothly. He was still plagued by the petty jealousies of some of his peers, and increasingly these were being voiced as outright complaints and criticisms. His youth aroused the jealousy of a Colonel Robert Gillespie, the Commander of the forces in Java, who felt that because Java had not been declared a King's Colony, he had lost his rightful position of Lieutenant-Governorship. Meanwhile, there was a constant exchange of communication with the East Indian Company in Calcutta, who were increasingly concerned by Raffles' heavy expenditure, which was unmatched by income.

The problems of government were completely overshadowed when, on 26 November 1814, Raffles' beloved wife Olivia died. He was distraught at this sudden loss, and on her cenotaph he inscribed the following verse:

> OH THOU WHOM NE'ER MY CONSTANT HEART
> ONE MOMENT HATH FORGOT
> THO' FATE SEVERE HATH BID US PART
> YET STILL FORGET ME NOT.

For ten years Olivia had stood at Raffles' side as he had made his way from Assistant Secretary in Penang to Lieutenant-Governor in Java. She had accompanied him on visits, hosted receptions, nursed him through illness, advised him, consoled him and clearly loved him. Now she was gone, leaving a void that Raffles would never fill.

Through the New Year he was grief-stricken, but then more bad news arrived. His friend and mentor Lord Minto had also died. Raffles' health seemed about to fail him completely – and it was in science that he found new strength and enthusiasm. First he determined to climb Gunong Gede, a mountain peak behind Batavia that had never been climbed by a European. This he achieved. Then he concerned himself with other matters of science and natural history – not least a major volcanic explosion on the distant island of Sumbawa.

Only by keeping his mind active in this way could he find the strength to continue. In his own words, he was '. . . a lonely man, like one that has long since been dead, but for whom activity and the cares of public responsibility are now almost necessary for existence'.

The journey from Bogor necessitated travelling for hundreds of miles along the tracks and pathways of the island. But hardship never daunted Raffles – indeed he seemed to thrive on it.

In April 1815, he decided that the time was appropriate for him to make a tour of the island – and, *en route* finally to see for himself the Hill of Statues described by Cornelius. He set off on 26 April, accompanied by a small party including Captain Baker and Lieutenant Thomas Watson, who later recalled: 'The road was in many places so steep as to render our progress in carriages somewhat tedious, and finding our horses themselves unable to advance, we had recourse to the assistance of a pair of buffaloes yoked by means of a long rope in front of the horses . . .'.

The American naturalist Dr Thomas Horsfield later wrote: 'This journey afforded Stamford an opportunity for examining in person those stupendous monumental remains of a hierarchy long since obsolete, which are promiscuously scattered through all parts of the island. In the dominions of the native princes they exist, however, in greater abundance, and possess a more important character.'

The progress across 400 miles of wild and wooded landscape was arduous and slow. But they were met on their way by welcoming villagers and accommodating chiefs and regents. At such stops Raffles took the opportunity to investigate the

Java was, and remains, extraordinarily beautiful. Volcanic explosions have, over the centuries, provided highly fertile soils that are abundent in foliage. It took Raffles ten years working as a clerk in London to be posted to Southeast Asia, but once he arrived, he never wanted to return home.

results of his land reform ideas, as well as his moves to introduce and improve vaccinations for Java's population. On 8 May he wrote:

> . . . we performed a long and arduous journey of nearly fifty miles through the forest of Dayu-luhur, a route which has never before been attempted by Europeans. On leaving Maganang the road entered at once into a thick forest of bamboos, which grow in clumps at some distance from each other, leaving the space between perfectly unoccupied by any kind of vegetation. At a considerable height the trees branch off and meet, giving a mutual support and forming a canopy so close and thick as to exclude the light at mid-day.

This difficult' journey continued for another ten days, until, on 18 May 1815, Raffles first saw Borobudur. He was awestruck.

He had always felt that something grand and significant must have existed in the past, and here it was. As he said in his address to the Batavian Society of Arts and Sciences later that year, 'We are at a loss whether most to admire the extent and grandeur of the whole construction, or the beauty, richness and correctness of the sculpture.'

Raffles was a man out of his own time. He had a large breadth of vision, and the ability to resist the influence of social opinion around him. He didn't mind if he was considered a renegade or an oddball, and most of his sympathies do seem much more democratic and anthropological than anything else expressed at that time. But when he heard the reports from Cornelius of some large structure, he would still have had a difficult time trying to understand what it was that these pieces of stone jutting out of the earth would have portended. He had a very empirical cast of mind, and didn't jump to conclusions. He would never accept stories without testing them. He was also very methodical, and was no doubt prepared to be disappointed, as most archaeologists are. Nine times out of ten such stories are widely exaggerated. But not this time. Raffles was stupefied by the sheer presence of Borobudur.

> Boro Bodo is admirable as a majestic work of art. The great extent of the masses of building covered in some parts with the luxuriant vegetation of the climate, the beauty and delicate execution of the separate portions, the symmetry and regularity of the whole, the great number and interesting character of the statues and reliefs, with which they are ornamented, excite our wonder that they were not earlier examined, sketched and described.

When Raffles actually arrived at Borobudur and was able to compare the regularity, the size of this structure with what he had seen in the past, he was extremely excited. Because he was actually eager to find traces of a new civilization, he was one of the few people who would have been able to recognize them if he saw them. And this was the first time that anything of such a monumental nature had ever been reported in the whole of Southeast Asia. Not just Indonesia or Java, but the whole enormous region. The discovery had been made in an unlikely place – many would have expected to find it a lot closer to India, rather than in an island in the ocean far off the mainland of Asia. It must have confirmed Raffles' suspicions that there had been a pretty advanced civilization in this region at some remote period of antiquity.

Raffles, however, had no real means of knowing how long ago that was. One can imagine how many other questions he would also have had in his mind and been intrigued by. It must have pained him to realize that he probably would never be able to answer some of them in his lifetime. At the same time, he fully intended to try to answer them as best he could. As a man of science, he was both thrilled and perplexed: the questions were there before him: what exactly was it for? Who had built it? How had they had built it ? And, of course, ultimately, why had it been abandoned?

The early dawn is the finest time to view Borobudur, as it rises majestically above the surrounding plane like a mountain. It must have been an extraordinary sight to ancient pilgrims.

The Riddle of the Lost Temple

'Nothing can exceed the air of melancholy, desolation, and ruin, which this spot presents; and the feelings of every visitor must be forcibly in unison with the scene of surrounding devastation, when he reflects upon the origin of this once venerated, hallowed spot; the seat and proof of the perfection of arts no longer in existence in Java . . . the patronage and encouragement which the arts and sciences must have received, and the inexhaustible wealth and resources which the Javanese of those times must have possessed!'

WHAT WAS IT FOR?

Referring to both Prambanan and Borobudur, Raffles expressed his delight and fascination at what he saw:

The ruins of these two places are admirable as majestic works of art. The great extent of the masses of building covered in some parts with the luxuriant vegetation of the climate, the beauty and delicate execution of the separate portions, the symmetry and regularity of the whole, the great number and interesting character of the statues and bas-reliefs, with which they are ornamented, excite our wonder that they were not earlier examined, sketched and described.

My object is to collect the raw materials then to establish any system of my own; and notwithstanding I have in some instances assumed something of a hypothesis I am by no means wedded to it or bound to support it.

It apparently took 200 men two weeks to clear the overgrowth of jungle from the temple. Even then, as this illustration shows, tall trees grew from the terraces. The presence of trees suggest that the whole monument must have been obscured.

What Raffles saw before him, when the clearing work he had ordered revealed the monument in its entirety – although the terraces were often still full of soil and some trees – was a pyramid with a base 370 feet by 370 feet square. It is built on a natural hill and thus has no interior. Above four square terraces, there were three circular terraces. The sides of the first four levels have galleries of reliefs – totalling 1460 in number – that cover the sides. On the uppermost levels there were 72 perforated stupas, each enclosing an image of a seated Buddha. These were arranged around a central stupa.

Borobudur has fascinated John Miksic, the archaeologist, for years:

It's an intellectual puzzle. Here are the various forms of data that we have, but we don't have any direct writing about the site, we don't have any inscriptions which tell us any of the

basic information like who built the place, why they built it, when was it done. All this has to be inferred from clues that anybody can see. So you can start off with just the bare fact that here's this big mountain of stone. And then you can go and look at the different things that we do know about it, bring in other contextual information from other temples nearby – the style of the sculptures, the inscriptions that relate to other sites in the vicinity, the little bit of archaeological research that was done on the site and so on – and say this is how

we're gradually building up a picture. Starting off with a period when nobody even knew for sure whether it was Buddhist or Hindu, you can then go on and present it as a kind of gradually evolving solution to an intellectual problem, which anybody still has a right to draw their own conclusions about. No one can prove to a very high degree of certainty that their explanation is any better than anybody else's.

After the UNESCO reconstruction, some of the Buddhas on the upper level were left uncovered. Their serenity and poise are as apparent today as when first sculpted over a thousand years ago.

Raffles had shown a keen interest in Javanese history and had commissioned a team of Javanese scholars to translate ancient Javanese texts. But he was starting from a clean slate as far as discovering what the origins of Borobudur were. He was able to make some suppositions based on the evidence before him, and wrote later, in his *History of Java*: 'I shall simply observe that it seems to be the general opinion of those most versed in Indian antiquities that the . . . temple . . . [was] . . . sacred to the worship of [Buddha] . . .'

In September 1815, in his address to the Batavian Society of Arts and Sciences, Raffles spoke about the ruins he had seen.

These extensive ruins lay claim to the highest antiquity; and, considering the vicinity of the temples to have been the seat of the earliest monarchy in Java, I may be permitted, in the words of Captain Baker, to lament the contrast of the present times, with 'times long since past'. 'Nothing,' he observes, 'can exceed the air of melancholy, desolation, and ruin, which this spot presents; and the feelings of every visitor must be forcibly in unison with the scene of surrounding devastation, when he reflects upon the origin of this once venerated, hallowed spot; the seat and proof of the perfection of arts no longer in existence in Java . . . the patronage and encouragement which the arts and sciences must have received, and the inexhaustible wealth and resources which the Javanese of those times must have possessed!'

Raffles continues to quote Baker's observations: 'Never have I met with such stupendous, laborious and finished specimens of human labour, and of the polished, refined taste of ages long since forgot, and crowded together in so small a compass . . .' Raffles added: 'I have preferred giving you the words of Captain

Baker, while the subject was fully impressed on his mind, and while in the midst of the objects which he contemplated – there is a feeling excited at such a moment that gives a colouring to the picture, and which is weakened in the faded tints of a more distant view.'

Referring specifically to Borobudur, Raffles commented: 'The ruins of Boro Bodo may be ranked as remarkable for grandeur in design, peculiarity of style, and exquisite workmanship . . . The figures and costume are evidently Indian; and we are at a loss whether most to admire the extent and grandeur of the whole construction, or the beauty, richness and correctness of the sculpture.'

Raffles had picked up the name 'Boro Bodo' from locals but had little idea as to its meaning. Indeed, people have argued about the derivation of the name Borobudur ever since it was first known in the early nineteenth century. There is a fourteenth-century reference to Budur, but we don't know if that means Borobudur or not. There are no Javanese words such as Boro or Budur, so the word presumably is some kind of corruption of another language. It could originate from a corruption of a phrase found in a Javanese inscription: the Sanskrit phrase 'Bhumisambhara budara'. The last part, 'budara', could have become Borobudur. The phrase itself means 'The Mountain of accumulation of Merit on the ten stages of the Bodhisattva'. Mountains play a key role in Javanese thought, and here merit could be accumulated by traversing the ten stages (a popular Buddhist belief) on the course towards becoming a Bodhisattva. There are many sects of Buddhism, and the Javanese of the early ninth century are known to have practised a form of Buddhism known as 'Mahayana'. This form of Buddhism believed in a stage prior to becoming a Buddha; this was the stage of being a Bodhisattva – an enlightened being who chooses to stay on earth and help others rather than going on to the state known as Nirvana. The logic behind associating the Bhumisambhara budara with Borobudur is that – as will be described – one has to pass through ten clearly defined stages to reach the top of the temple and attain enlightenment.

The personality of this relief has led some to believe it may be a representation of the king – or one of the kings – who sponsored Borobudur. The detail is striking – notice the folds in the neck.

THE FIRST LEVEL AND BUDDHISM

Borobudur's reliefs – all 1460 of them – are not only a record of Javanese life, Buddhist teaching and devotion but also a highly advanced form of narrative art. The way the scenes are composed and the way the carvers have experimented with things like perspective are quite extraordinary. The characters in the reliefs are never static; there is always movement, always a feeling of action. This was a period when pictorial art in most of the world was still very two-dimensional. The art in these reliefs can arguably be considered the most highly developed of its kind at that time anywhere in the world.

There are, in fact, five levels of reliefs and the builders intended the lowest level to be visible to all. These are images of ordinary village people doing ordinary things – and of the punishments in hell for their misdemeanours. Adulterers, thieves and murderers are flayed alive or burnt to death. It is pointedly directed at the humble villager to remind him or her to keep to the 'right' and avoid the 'wrong' ways of behaving. Behind the moral lessons of these reliefs one can also see an enormous degree of detail of everyday life – what the Javanese wore, used for cooking, used as homes, and so forth. It is quite unique, and how sad it is that Raffles never got to see what are in some ways the most impressive and revealing of all the reliefs. For, during construction – for reasons explained later – these reliefs were covered up. They were only rediscovered a century ago.

The hidden reliefs are the best visual account that exists of ancient Javanese society. The lowest level of reliefs may have been designed primarily to keep the villagers in check, but they now provide us with fascinating insight into how the people lived, dressed and behaved.

By ascending the staircase, we come upon the first of the levels that *would* have been visible to pilgrims in the past and continues to be visible to us today. There are four series of reliefs on this first level – two on either side – and within them one can, for example, see in great detail an account of the life of Buddha.

These reliefs show Buddha – Siddhartha Gautama – being born about 2500 years ago, around 560 BC. He grew up as an Indian prince and lived in great luxury until, at the age of 29, he renounced his life of indolence and set out to seek solutions to the problems of human suffering. Beyond his father's palace he was moved to pity by the suffering of the poor; during one trip alone he saw a weak old man, a fatally sick man, a corpse and an ascetic monk. Siddhartha Gautama left his past behind him and set out to seek the answer to such destitution.

Siddhartha Gautama sought enlightenment and, after a long period of reflection seated under a Banyan tree, he achieved it. He came to the conclusion that there were 'Four Holy Truths'. These were that 'All life is suffering', 'All suffering is the result of lust and desire', 'The removal of desire leads to the removal of suffering' and 'The way to deliverance is through the Eightfold Path of righteous belief, righteous intention, righteous word, righteous conduct, righteous living,

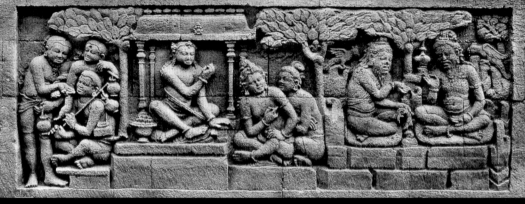

righteous effort, righteous thinking, righteous meditation'. The Sanskrit for Enlightened One is 'Buddha', and thus a new religion was established.

At the time of Buddhism's widest dissemination, (by about the year 1000), it extended from India, the land of its origin, and Sri Lanka right through Southeast and East Asia as far as Japan. There is no doubt that there was a sense in which Buddhists in all those different countries felt that they belonged to a religious community. Although beliefs differed slightly from country to country, and even between regions, there seems to have been a general belief that Buddha himself was unapproachable, having alrady passed into non-existence. However, there were other, intermediary, beings along the path to Nirvana who could still be called upon, and it appears that in every Buddhist country there was a kind of ancillary division of supernatural beings. Some called them gods, others called them enlightened beings; they were higher than humans, but they were still in some way contactable and they could intercede on your behalf.

The core of Buddhism is always the same, no matter what the sect. It is basically a release from suffering, an acknowledgement that the root of suffering is action and the attachment to desire, the desire for worldly things. Beyond that point Buddhism diverges into many different sects which have very different ideas about how long it takes to reach the goal of enlightenment, ranging from a multitude of lifetimes to a single lifetime. They also differ about whether or not it is possible to use various artificial techniques, including buildings such as Borobudur, statues, chants and mantras and other kinds of designs, in order to obtain enlightenment very quickly.

The idea that one could achieve enlightenment in a single lifetime by using appropriate techniques was a relatively recent one – dating from perhaps AD 600 – and naturally it had a major impact on Buddhist art and architecture. Buildings such as Borobudur could have been designed, constructed and employed to speed up the process of achieving enlightenment.

These doctrines initially developed within India alone, but very gradually began to filter both south towards Sri Lanka and north towards the Himalayas. At the same time, trade routes were beginning to open up between India and islands such as Java, and a great many of the traders and travellers on these arduous and long journeys were Buddhists.

THE SPREAD OF BUDDHISM

The history of Buddhism's spread would have been barely known to Raffles. He would have found it hard to say how it was that if, as he felt, the temple was

The easiest reliefs to comprehend are those that depict the life of Buddha. In this relief, Siddhartha Gautama has left his father's palace and ventured out into the world beyond. What he sees distresses him – and changes his life.

Buddhist, the religion had spread from India over 3000 miles to a small island in Southeast Asia; and why it was that on this island there had been built the largest Buddhist monument in the world.

There developed a Buddhist realm, a kind of Buddhist sphere of interaction that covered a huge area, possibly as a result of the persecution of Buddhists in India. So, by the fourth century AD, at about the time of the Roman Emperor Constantine, there was an impressive network of trade routes and monasteries from India to Afghanistan and Pakistan, all the way across China and into Southeast Asia, although it was still relatively limited. Five hundred years later, by the eighth and ninth centuries, Buddhism formed an even denser network of alliances going all the way to Japan, and it is obvious that people did make use of those connections to travel and also to do business.

Buddhism was the first unifying element that brought large parts of Asia together in a mutually intelligible framework of communication. Pilgrims were travelling to the holy areas of India, and large numbers of people from China, Japan and Southeast Asia were drawn there to see the various sights mentioned in the Buddhist texts. Buddhism would have spurred a whole new wave of communication and exchange of ideas.

As the trade networks of Southeast Asia flourished, so, along with cotton, spices, woods and metals, came religion. It is assumed that it was around the fifth and sixth centuries AD, when the sea routes began to flourish (as opposed to the mainland routes), that Buddhism and Hinduism spread from India and the mainland to islands such as Java. The archaeologist John Miksic is in no doubt about the intellectual and commercial effect of Buddhism and its unifying influence:

> Buddhism was the first real religion to knit together a large part of the earth's surface. By the first and second centuries AD, Buddhism was already making inroads into China; by the third and fourth centuries AD, there were Buddhists in Indonesia and no doubt the spaces in between such as mainland southeast Asia; and the overland route between India and China would have had large numbers of Buddhists along it. Buddhism provided for the first time a kind of shared set of meanings, even a shared language, and a network of contacts which then could be exploited both for expanding Buddhism itself and also for other purposes [such as commerce]. Buddhism is certainly favourably disposed towards commerce, and many of the early Buddhist travellers were in fact merchants as well. So, for the first time, it knitted together a large area of the earth both intellectually and also commercially.

In Java, between about AD 750 and 850, Buddhism certainly seems to have enjoyed a short but intense period of popularity. This when all the Buddhist temples – such as Borobudur – were built, and in this hundred-year period the Buddhists of Java clearly had high hopes for their religion. Borobudur is the most outstanding illustration of their ambition and ability.

THE BUDDHIST TEMPLE – FOR WHOM?

Debate still continues concerning who was actually allowed to use the temple – and how. Some, like John Miksic, believe there would have been several groups who used Borobudur in different ways. The general population probably never got further than the foot of the monument and did most of their worshipping by either walking round the base of it or by participating in other kinds of ceremony down at the foot of the hill. Others, like the historian John Villiers, contend that, as a representation of the Buddhist world, with its reliefs providing a complete textbook of the doctrines of Mahayana Buddhism, it must surely have been accessible to pilgrims from anywhere and of any class.

My own view is that human nature changes little, and that the impulse to make the terraces increasingly restricted must have been too great for the ruling hierarchy to resist. By being allowed to ascend the temple, they were marked out as special and distinct from the general public. Similarly, this was not a temple you could ascend rapidly – for some it must have taken years to achieve a full appreciation of the reliefs and thus be allowed to transfer from one terrace to the next until you reached the very top.

Those who were allowed to ascend thus continued on their way around the ten sets of reliefs (four on the first level, two on each of the three subsequent square levels).

SUBSEQUENT LEVELS

Those allowed on to the terraces were confronted with work that is absolutely extraordinary. Even today the craft and skill of the reliefs is quite breath-taking. One begins at the lowest levels and walks clockwise, viewing the first set of reliefs. Then, after one complete circumambulation, one begins to view the next set. The four lower levels are bordered by an exterior wall that creates a series of narrow galleries, which for the ancient pilgrim would have precluded exterior views. Each side of the monument has a staircase that ascends directly to the top, but one can presume that where the staircase crossed a gallery it would have been gated or screened in some way.

Even today, Buddhist monks feel inspired by the work of their religious ancestors. Sri Pannewayo, the abbot of the nearby Mendut monastery, is moved each

The quality and finesse
of this carving is superb.
The men on this ship
all have character,
movement and humour –
notice the sailor holding
onto the anchor.

time he processes through the galleries: '. . . Every time, every moment I see Borobudur, my faith in Buddha's teaching increases... when we observe the reliefs, we also can learn about the building in ancient times, daily life in ancient times, religious life in ancient times and the beauty of art one thousand two hundred years ago.'

Once again, it is the anthropologist John Miksic who seems to have interpreted the reliefs most successfully. As he explains, it is the practice today to divide the monument from bottom to top into three stages, corresponding to the three stages in Buddhist thought on the way to Nirvana. According to this interpretation, the first category is the *Kamadhatu* – the 'Realm of Desire'. This represents man before he has acquired a sense of morality, and is depicted in the already mentioned 'hidden texts' at the bottom of the temple. The 160 panels of these reliefs illustrate a text called *Mahakarmavibhangga*, concerning the laws of cause and effect, action and punishment.

The second stage is known as the *Rupadhatu* – the 'Realm of Forms'. This illustrates the period in which man is becoming more enlightened concerning the meaning of life. Here the novice monk or lay person could receive instruction relating to the need to sacrifice oneself for others, and the ultimate reward for righteous behaviour, which was the release from rebirth. This realm is thought to be represented in the four-sided galleries which contain narrative reliefs along both their inner and outer walls.

These narratives begin in the middle of the east side of the temple and run clockwise around the monument. To follow them, you must start at the eastern stairway and turn to the left, keeping the monument always to your right. Such a circumambulation, or *pradaskina*, formed a major part of Buddhist worship. By following the stories depicted one accumulates merit simply by the act of walking. In order to follow all ten narratives in sequence (four on the first level, followed by two on each of the three subsequent levels), one must walk around the monument ten times – a total distance of almost 3 miles.

As one enters the gallery on the first level, two series of reliefs, one above the other, are visible on the inner wall of the balustrade to the left. These depict episodes from the *Jakata* tales, a collection of stories regarding the lives of Buddha before he became a human.

To one's right, on the main wall of the first gallery, are two more series of reliefs. Those in the upper series are the most significant, and are devoted to the life story of the historical Buddha. The narrative follows an ancient text known as the *Lalitavistara* – 'The Unfolding of the Play'.

The lowest level is actually a massive stone girdle that had to be hastily built during construction to prevent the temple collapsing.

The first panel in this series shows Buddha in heaven. In the next scene, he informs the assembled deities that he will be born as a human. The next five panels concern activities in heaven. In panel 8 we see Queen Maya, Buddha's future mother, with her husband King Suddhodana in the palace. Homage is then paid to Buddha, and the next reliefs depict his descent to earth in the form of a white elephant; the queen discussing her dream about the elephant; and various episodes leading to Queen Maya's journey to the Lumbini Park in preparation for Buddha's birth.

This sequence is followed by other familiar episodes in the life of Buddha: the archery tournament, Buddha's encounter with old age, sickness, death, and a monk; Gautama's escape from his father's palace; his cutting off of his hair, being attacked by the demon Mara, and then being tempted by Mara's daughters. We see Buddha's enlightenment; his crossing of the Ganges; the the first sermon in the Deer Park at Benares. Finally, back at the original starting point at the eastern stairway, the story ends.

The lower reliefs on the main wall depict more *Jakata* tales. The first shows a prince who married a nymph. In one panel nymphs are taking water from a pool; in another panel the prince and his spouse are serenaded.

In total, there were 504 Buddhas and Bodhisattvas. Not all survive but many do, holding the same position they've had for centuries. Those in niches may represent hermits in mountain caves.

On the next terrace begins a new story which takes up most of the rest of the reliefs. This is the *Gandavyuha*, the account of a merchant by the name of Sudhana who made a pilgrimage in search of spiritual knowledge. The *Gandavyuha* material occupies almost 500 panels, many of which are quite similar. They represent Sudhana and the various teachers whom he encounters on his pilgrimage, each of whom offers him guidance. The object of this series was to instruct and edify rather than to entertain; the reliefs tend to be repetitive; and the last set of panels on the fourth terrace illustrates the *Bhadracari*, a sequel to the *Gandhavyuha*.

Set atop the balustrade walls surrounding the four relief galleries are 432 Buddha statues set into niches. The hand posture or *mudra* of the Buddhas on each side of the monument is different, except at the top level, where a fifth *mudra* is shown on all four sides. These *mudras* and their directions correspond to a system of *dhyani* Buddhas, each with a specific name. The Buddha of the east is known as Aksobhya; on the south is Ratnasambhava; on the west, Amitabha, and on the north, Amoghasidda. The Buddha positioned on the top wall, Vairocana, is the guardian of the centre or zenith.

The third and highest stage of Borobudur is called the *Arupadhatu* – the 'Realm

of Formlessness'. This term is applied to the three uppermost levels of the monument, with their stupas enclosing Buddha images. It is thought that upon reaching this level, having absorbed the instruction of the various teachers portrayed throughout the lower galleries, the pilgrim would no longer be in any need of external guidance.

All that remained was to complete the last steps of the journey at one's own pace. The pilgrim now understood that the pictures below, like everything else in the visible world, were illusory. The pilgrim had successfully accomplished the three stages: the first level where man is influenced by negative desires; the second level, where man can control his desires; and the highest level, where man is no longer bound by such physical desires.

As each level is accessible to smaller and smaller numbers of people, only a very small portion of the élite would have been allowed up to the highest level. Although this is highly debated, it does seem that Borobudur was built at a time when the rituals of the Javanese élite were becoming increasingly distinct from those of the masses. It seems sensible to assume that same élite would have kept the privilege of reaching the top to themselves.

And reaching the top was – and is – a privilege. Even today, after only an hour or two of viewing the reliefs, one feels, on leaving behind the enclosed levels and arriving at the top, an enormous sense of space and opening. The temple sits at the heart of a wide plain, lavish in green palm and banana groves. Here and there a trickle of smoke winds lazily skywards. In the distance the gracious volcanoes sit, as if in judgement. The sense of space, nature, light and air is overwhelming. Surely this was the builders' intention – their visual equivalent of reaching Nirvana. Surely, too, this is the reward for persisting with the study of 1460 complicated reliefs in the search for enlightenment. These top three levels are made up of three concentric circles. There are no more corners or harsh angles – only smooth lines, unbroken and tranquil.

Javanese Buddhism was probably closest to modern Tibetan Buddhism. The similarity is that both are tantric. Evolved from beliefs in magic, Tantric Buddhism helped believers to more quickly achieve enlightenment through the use of medicines, exercise and performance, such as dance. Over the years, this form of Buddhism was refined and developed and certain beliefs within it came to be seen as of a higher order and for the select few only. It was felt that these higher categories of belief needed no icons, in other words, they were abstract in form. Perhaps that is why Borobudur has no illustrations on the final three circular levels. Most importantly, this is the site of 72 perforated stupas. Inside each and every one is a seated Buddha – as poised and contemplative now as when first carved over a thousand years ago.

It is the nature of these stupas that makes one feel that the top must have had restricted access – these perforated stupas made it impossible to see the images unless you were very close to them. Those outside the monument could not view them. This also suggests that only the religious priests and those lay people – such as kings – who were believed to have generated enough spiritual power were allowed to the top, where they were considered as worthy of being allowed to sit next to the stupas and see the actual Buddhas inside them.

There are also many theories concerning Borobudur's representation of the 'Buddhist world'. Is it a Mandala reflecting the Buddhist Cosmos? Numerology too is much discussed – how important a part did that play at the time? Much of this remains undeciphered – why are there 72 stupas at the top? Why 504 Buddha heads? Could it be because the digits add up to nine – a holy Buddhist number? We don't know and probably never will. All we can conclude is that the structure is wholly individual and what it represents is unique in the Buddhist world.

The 1460 relief panels, stretch for over three miles. Each character is individual, each story particular in some way.

We do know that elements of the temple, such as the perforated stupas, are unique. Indeed Borobudur is unusual in many ways, because its levels and reliefs are the things that really count. The central crowning stupa is but a pinnacle. It is the successful completion of the encyclopaedic reliefs that marks the successful journey of the monk. Borobudur is a monument designed for the intellect – and that is one of the key elements that makes it special.

ENLIGHTENMENT

The point of enlightenment at Borobudur was not for one's soul's self-gratification; it wasn't to then disappear into Nirvana, or non-existence, and 'not be' again. Instead, according to the Mahayana school of Buddhism, the theory was that once you had enlightenment yourself you could then become a kind of a saviour, you could spread it to all other beings, you could give the pleasure which comes from complete awareness to all other creatures.

Both Buddha and Bodhisattva come from the same root, 'Bodhi', which just means 'enlightened', while 'sattva' means 'being'. There are different ways of translating Bodhisattva, but 'enlightened being' is perhaps the most appropriate. When Guatama Siddhartha sat underneath the Bodhi tree and achieved enlightenment, he was a Bodhisattva, and because he was enlightening others and teaching he had not yet gone into Nirvana. Once he had actually entered

The monks from nearby Mendut Monastery only rarely come to the temple to pray. Special permission had to be granted for our filming. But when the monks do come, they make offerings of prayer, candles and orchids, then circumambulate the great stupa three times.

Nirvana he was a Buddha, lost to existence; his corporeal or his individual personal self no longer existing.

The whole ethos of the Borobudur system was to make you a Bodhisattva, not a Buddha. This meant that once you had achieved enlightenment you voluntarily held yourself back from going into Nirvana, into 'non-being'. So Borobudur's purpose is really to prepare you, not to cease existing, but to become a kind of saint. One could remain in existence as long as one wanted to – that way indeed you could avoid ever becoming a non-being. The idea of becoming a Buddha before others do is actually frowned upon and scorned by this Mahayana Buddhism, which Borobudur espouses. Those who, as soon as they become enlightened, immediately enter Nirvana – ceasing to exist – and therefore don't pass on their wisdom to other beings, are considered selfish. Borobudur's religious purpose was thus to make people into teachers.

THE CENTRAL STUPA?

Even today on the rare occasions that Buddhist monks are allowed on to the monument to pray, it is a moment of great spiritual significance for them. But what is it that they are praying to? The central stupa is empty – do modern monks pray to what may once have been inside?

One theory is that Buddha's ashes were divided into eight and deposited in eight holy sites of the Buddhist world – including Borobudur. There is, however, no convincing evidence for this.

It is possible, however, that there was some kind of ritual deposit in the main stupa at Borobudur. Certainly there are two cavities visible in the main stupa – long empty, of course. All the smaller stupas around it seem to have contained some sort of deposit, which was probably the attraction for the looters who rifled them. The idea of having a relic in the centre of the stupa is something that is found in many other Buddhist temples in the world, including those in Southeast Asia, in places like Thailand and Burma. But there is no reference in any of the ancient Indonesian inscriptions to relics of Buddha ever having been brought to Indonesia. Nor are there references to the use of the ashes of dead monks, which still occurs today in Thailand. There, when monks are cremated, their ashes are mixed with clay and made into small model stupas which are distributed to devotees. There is no literary evidence to suggest that anything like that was ever done in Indonesia.

Perhaps there is a clue in the fact that the central stupa at Borobudur is constructed without any sort of clean open space. It had a fine outer shell, but inside it was not as neat as you would expect if it were meant to be a holy container for a relic. One would also have expected a high-quality statue inside the chamber, as relics are almost always associated with some particular image. In fact only one image, a damaged one, was apparently found inside that stupa. A more likely theory is that the statue was damaged in the construction and simply incorporated into the building because any holy image, even if it was faulty, was thought already to have a spark of divinity in it.

Of course, under the stone layers of the monument there remains the natural hill, so it is theoretically possible that buried under that soil might be something that was interred a long time ago. We will probably never know.

CHAPTER

WHO BUILT IT?

*The point is to trace from whence those rude and savage tribes received their first rudiments
of civilization: whether from Egypt or the colonies established by that power, or at a
subsequent period from an Indian country, may be a matter of doubt, but that they were early
visited by traders from. . . India seems established on incontrovertible evidence.*

RAFFLES, QUOTED IN LADY SOPHIA RAFFLES' MEMOIR

Having returned to Bogor, Raffles continued to wonder about Borobudur.
Just who, for example, had actually built this enormous monument?
'The antiquities of Java afford such ample and interesting subject for
speculation that I shall presume . . . for some opinion concerning their origin,' he
wrote in his *History of Java*. 'The style and ornament of this temple are found
much to resemble those of . . . the continent of India.'

His Resident at Yogyakarta was John Crawfurd, who also believed in an Indian
origin: 'The scenery, the figures, the faces, and costume are not native, but those
of Western India. Of human figures, the faces are characterized by the strongest
features of the Hindu countenance . . . At the moment in which these temples
were constructed, there is ground to believe that a body of emigrants must have
arrived from India.'

Raffles would have had little evidence to work with. He would have seen no
inscriptions on the stone and read few accounts from the period. He could only
guess from what he already knew. Not surprisingly, his thoughts focused on India,
over 2000 miles away. The similarities seemed too great to ignore. Even Raffles
had trouble imagining that the Javanese had built the temple themselves – surely
it must have been a dynasty that had sailed to Java or, at the very least, Indian
craftsmen in the employ of a rich Javanese king.

Over the past two centuries, our knowledge has greatly improved, thanks to
the work of people like Jan Wisseman-Christie at the University of Hull. We
can now presume that temple building, along with state expansion, began in

100

earnest in about AD 750 with the Candis (temples) at Kalasan, then Sewu, then Ploasan, all in Central Java. These were both Buddhist and Hindu temples. Borobudur began shortly thereafter. From the 820s to the 880s the state expanded with increasing international trade. A system of coinage and weights and measures was standardized and communicated to trading partners in the archipelago.

Like Raffles, some have felt that the social order that constructed Borobudur must have been foreign. But today we can say with some assurance that this is now an outdated idea. Borobudur was built by the Javanese. Indonesia does have large stone monuments dating back to the prehistoric period, and while it is clear that Borobudur and others were influenced by Indian models – and of course by Hinduism and Buddhism, with which they were connected – it is also clear that the influences came not only from Indian traders and monks coming to Java but from Javanese travelling to India. We know that Indian architectural texts were imported by the Javanese at the time (Sanskrit terminology was used for specialist discussions) and that although Indian teachers came to Java in the late eighth century, Javanese traders, pilgrims and religious students frequently travelled to India. The Javanese were outwardly connected, having traded in Southeast Asian waters since the Neolithic period, and across the Indian Ocean and South China Sea from at least as far back as the Iron Age. The Javanese were therefore very eclectic in their cultural and religious borrowings from abroad, and tended to adapt them to local needs and traditions.

These local needs and traditions largely revolved around the local kings, chiefs and sultans. It was their decisions regarding how to control their position or communicate with the gods that largely decided if, when and how a temple was built. It is quite clear that many of these local fiefs were very powerful. A quote from an Arab geographer Abu Zaid in AD 916 regarding Java illustrates the breadth of authority exercised by one such 'Maharaja':

The authority of the Maharaja [of Zubai] is exercised over these various islands, and the island in which he resides is extremely fertile, and patches of habitation succeed each other without interruption. . . In effect there are no uninhabited places in the country and no ruins. He who comes into the country when he is on a journey if he is mounted he may go wherever he pleases; if he is tired or if his mount is in difficulty in carrying on, then he may stop wherever he pleases.

The social structure appears to have been pyramidal. On the highest level sat the royal officials, who lived in villages, had titles, had military or police to guard tax revenue (e.g. rice). Then came the landed nobility, then tax collectors, then the religious authorities, and finally the peasants. The men ploughed, felled trees, hunted, smithied, built houses, worshipped in formal temples and worked for the king. The women planted, harvested, cooked, wove, made pottery and marketed.

From archaeological sources we know a fair amount about the layout of villages on the Kedu plain around Borobudur in the year 800 or so. There are about thirty other known sites from the Borobudur period including a fair number of smaller temples, almost all of them Hindu, so it seems that around Borobudur at that time there must have been around twenty or thirty small villages. Among them was distributed a large population, many of whom prob-

The blocks of volcanic andesite would possibly have been provisionally carved where the block was found, before being transported to the site for a more expert craftsman to position and finish.

ably were still practising Hinduism. But given the way the Javanese have always tended to view religion, the commoners probably didn't differentiate very much between Hinduism and Buddhism. There was a very large monastic complex on the south side of the hill, which was probably quarters for monks and pilgrims. The hill itself it seems has a little extension up towards the northwest, and the remains of wooden structures, including copper nails, have been found there. Copper nails obviously were a rarity – expensive at any point in history – so they would have been for some impor-tant wooden structure.

While the priesthood would have been very concerned to empha-size the differences between Hinduism and Buddhism, the commoners probably would not have thought of themselves as being either Hindus or Buddhists – but rather as worshippers of Supreme Deities. So the people in these villages around Borobudur would have gone sometimes to a Hindu temple, and sometimes to Borobudur.

The dominant Royal Family at the time Borobudur was built seem to have styled themselves by the Sanskrit word 'Sailendra', which is a variant of a common phrase meaning 'The Lords of the Mountain'. It is unknown exactly what Sailendra meant in terms of a kind of ruling clan or a clique. It is thought that the Javanese did not have strong lineages – there never seems to have been a real hereditary system of kinship in historical times in Java. As far as one can tell, whenever a king died or was incapacitated there was a conference among the other nobles and someone would be chosen to become the next ruler. In the absence of a hereditary right to rule, it seems that there was probably an allied group of people who called themselves the Lords of the Mountain.

The other group at this time was called the Sanjaya, who distinguished themselves from the Buddhist Sailendra by being Hindu. The Lords of the Mountain and the Sanjaya seem to have co-operated in many ways. We know that the Sanjaya did donate to the construction of a number of Buddhist sites such as Kalassaan, which was built in around AD 778. We don't have any proof that they donated to Borobudur, but it could be assumed to have been the case. There is certainly evidence that they saw themselves as complementary opposites rather than foes.

THE WORLD AT THIS TIME

When Borobudur was built in the eighth and ninth centuries, Java could legitimately claim to be one of the world's leading civilizations. Europe had entered the 'Dark Ages' after the fall of Rome in the West. It was a time when there was hardly anybody left alive in Europe who could even read or write, except for the people in the monasteries. Basically all of the knowledge of classical European civilization had died out. Centuries would pass before it was recovered – mainly from the Arab world, when the Europeans regained some of the Greek classics in Arabic translation. While the Javanese were building great stone monuments, the Europeans were constructing in wood – it would be some time before anything as grand as a major stone cathedral was constructed.

At the same time, in South America, one well-known empire was in decline. The Mayan Empire in Central America was the first great classical empire in the Americas. It had begun its classical era in about the third century AD but it was coming to an end at just about the time Borobudur was built.

India at this time was relatively disorganized, the Gupta having been the last major empire, which ended in about the sixth century. After that time there was a period where the country was divided into several different kingdoms, although, given the size of India, each of these were of course fairly large, with a large population and resources to draw on. And there were several major Buddhist kingdoms, one of which was up in the Northeast around modern Bangladesh. It is believed that there were Indonesian monks who went to live in the monasteries there, a result no doubt of trade with the Bengal area. Down in South India, Madras was the centre of another kingdom, which had some important Buddhist sites associated with it.

There were probably very few Indians actually resident in Southeast Asia at any one time. There was almost no influence from any Indian everyday language in any of the languages of Southeast Asia – very little Tamil influence, for example, and almost no Bengali. The only major language of India to make an impact on the region was Sanskrit, which by this time was already a dead language in India, only used in texts and in rituals. It was mainly through the medium of scholarship and through literary sources, therefore, that Indian culture made its impact on this region, which means that what the Southeast Asians absorbed from India was what they took voluntarily. Indian culture provided a lot of metaphors that they could use to express ideas that they already had, but in more concrete and more meaningful form.

China's Tong dynasty, between AD 618 and 906 was, some say, the greatest period in the country's history. This is when the silk route was at is height. Chinese art at this time was very much open to outside influences – one thinks of all those terracotta figurines of westerners leading camels, on horseback and so forth. Generally speaking, apart from a few official emissaries and monks, most Chinese were forbidden to go outside China. There seems to be little evidence of Chinese passing through Southeast Asia at this time. However, Java was looked up to by many of the other kingdoms, including the Chinese themselves; they write that Java was one of the four great kingdoms of the world in the period when Borobudur was built.

MARITIME TRADE

The probability [is] that the rich productions of the Spice Islands would have been the first to excite the cupidity of Indian traders, in the same manner as they were subsequently the first to attract the attention of European speculators.

LETTER FROM RAFFLES TO WILLIAM MARSDEN,
QUOTED IN LADY SOPHIA RAFFLES' MEMOIRS

With the movement between India and China, Java became increasingly important as a port and trading post. Above all, the greatest profits came from spices. It is a quirk of nature that in one tiny spot on earth there is a grouping of what have become known as 'the Spice Islands'. These islands to the east of Java – the Moluccas and Banda islands – were the only source for condiments such as nutmeg, mace and cloves. For centuries spices, in particular pepper (which, strictly speaking, is not a fine spice) had been as valuable as gold. The Goths demanded ransoms in pepper, the Egyptians sent out expeditions to find cinnamon embalming and Roman emperors bribed voters with spice. In the absence of refrigeration, meat had to be heavily seasoned to hide the taste of decay, especially during the winter. The hotter the country, the

The surrounding volcanic plain of palms and groves provides the ideal setting for the simple curves and absence of reliefs that one finds on the final levels. This seems a deliberate attempt to visualize enlightenment.

spicier the food. Spice therefore became the great commodity of the growing maritime trade.

As the historian John Villiers explains: 'The trading pattern of Southeast Asia and indeed of the Indian Ocean to the west of Southeast Asia and of the South China Sea to the north and east, was extremely complex, but this huge maritime area formed the base of a unified trading system. It consisted entirely of relatively short-haul traders, forming an immensely long and complicated chain.'

In the first centuries after Christ, Graeco-Roman traders in southern India wrote of non-Indian ships (probably from Java and Sumatra) bringing pepper and spices from the East. The Roman author Pliny wrote: 'They bring [spices] over vast seas on rafts which have no rudders to steer them or oars to push. . . or sails or other aids to navigation. . . but instead only the spirit of man and human courage. . . Cinnamon is the chief object of their journey, and they say that these merchant sailors take almost five years before they return, and that many perish.'

In the fifth century AD a Chinese monk called Fâ-Hien wrote an account of such sea voyages:

> The great ocean spreads out, a boundless expanse. There is no knowing east or west; only by observing the sun, moon and stars was it possible to go forward. If the weather were dark and rainy, [the ship] went as she was carried by the wind, without any definite course. In the darkness of the night, only the great waves were to be seen, breaking on one another, and emitting a brightness like that of fire, with huge turtles and other monsters of the deep [all about]. The merchants were full of terror, not knowing where they were going. . . [And] on the sea there are many pirates, to meet with whom is speedy death. . . [But] after proceeding in this way for rather more than 90 days, the [ship] arrived at a country called Java. . .

By Raffles' era, however, things were changing. European demand for spice was in sharp decline, as fresh meat became available all year round. Moreover, the cost of maintaining fleets was proving extortionate and few countries could afford it. In 1770, a Frenchman, Pierre Poivre, Governor of Mauritius, smuggled out spices, cloves and nutmeg seedlings, to Zanzibar. And the British were equally active, establishing new spice plantations in West Sumatra and India. With the monopolies broken, prices fell further. It marked the end of 2000 years of intensive maritime trading which had made the area exceptionally wealthy and sought after. Without the income that the spice trade brought to Southeast Asia, it's probable that Borobudur would never have been built.

RICE

While spice was making the area rich, it was another commodity that brought Java – and in particular central Java – to prominence. That commodity was rice.

Central Java is one of the world's most fertile areas – its soils are full of volcanic nutrients – and rice has traditionally been its favoured crop. The Javanese must also have developed an excellent system of co-ordinating and controlling the supply of water to the populace to ensure good irrigation. The wealth of the Sailendra realm was based on the production of rice – the Sailendra kings grew wealthy by selling it to the coastal traders, who themselves were growing wealthy from spice. It also allowed the Sailendra to support, by the standards of the time, a very large population, and that in turn would have enabled them to build magnificent monuments.

Large and predictable harvests fixed the population in place. When successful, rice cultivation can produce a high enough yield to provide surplus to support large numbers of people who are not working as farmers for their major occupation.

Of course, it would be wrong to assume that rice production was particular to central Java. There are a number of other areas where the rice production can be as intensive as it is around Borobudur. East Java has long valleys, several of which can also support intensive rice production. There must have been other factors at work that helped to promote central Java, such as the development of a political system which could manipulate the surplus and actually turn it to some kind of centralized use which maybe other areas did not develop. Possibly the region's geography – a kind of enclosed basin shape – made it a bit more definable and controllable. Administrative systems therefore could have been set up which could tap all of the resources of this region more easily than if it was a spread out along linear river valleys.

STATEMENT OF POWER

There are few archaeological remains in Java from before the end of the seventh century. Anything earlier was probably Hindu and almost certainly made of wood that has long since decayed. The first stone temples were constructed during the eighth century high on the Dieng Plateau – the 'Place of the Gods'. Mountains were long held sacred by the Javanese. Spirits dwelt at the top of volcanoes, and Dieng is a perfect volcanic plain on which to build such monuments to religious humility. The very ground seeps with smoke and sulphur, mud pools bubble and hiss, lakes shimmer in green, red and yellow. It is not difficult to understand why,

High on a volcanic plain stand three small temples – probably the first to be built in the mid seventh century. The area is clouded in volcanic steam and mists. It is clear why this spot seemed so spiritual to the ancient Javanese.

according to Javanese thought, such areas are considered sources of ultimate truth and supernatural power.

The economic boom in Java seems to have reached a peak during the eighth century . The surplus of wealth to which the sale of rice contributed had made the ruling dynasties exceptionally rich. Needless to say, they were determined to make their position of power and control clear to everyone. Thus began the boom in temple building. The centre, particularly in the province of Kedu, proliferated with ever grander stone temples. We can assume that many have yet to be discovered and even rediscovered – some of those that were found in the nineteenth century have since disappeared. Estimates suggest there may have been over a hundred such buildings – most relatively small but some really quite ambitious. None, however, as far as we know, matched the staggering scale and grandeur of Borobudur.

We can assume that, like so many other aspiring monarchs, the ruling Sailendra sought to legitimize and thereby stabilize their position of power. They may therefore have looked to religion as a way of doing this. Hinduism and Buddhism, both, in origin, Indian religions, support the idea of the 'Raja' – a being halfway between ordinary man and the gods. This was clearly an appealing notion to these Javanese kings.

Since Buddhism claims to be a universal truth, equally applicable everywhere, then it follows that the religion should incorporate universal rulers. Indeed, there are many examples of these in Buddhism, starting with the Indian ruler Ashoka, in the third century BC. Focusing primarily on local cults and the caste system, Hinduism was much less useful to the Javanese kings, but it too has models of royalty, such as Rhama of the Rhamayana. By emulating these figures of religious power, the kings would have hoped to confirm their superiority over their people while offering them something spiritual at the same time. Such rulers believed that they had already become enlightened Bodhisattvas and therefore could inspire and guide other people to achieve higher levels of spiritual development. The temples built at this time, including Borobudur, were part of the rulers' attempts to both dominate and provide religious support to their subjects.

If one looks at Borobudur from the air, one could consider that it is a mandala, a formal representation of Buddhist cosmology. This is the symbolic idea which Buddhists – and indeed Hindus – have of the universe, the concept of the many different heavens fitting into each other and being surrounded by a circumambient ocean. At Borobudur the central column, the stupa, that goes down into the centre of the monument represents the cosmic axis that holds the whole universe together. It is important to remember that Southeast Asian rulers, including the Sailendra, aspired to be in a spiritual sense rulers of the entire cosmological universe. So the centre of their state temple was both spiritually the centre of their realm and a symbolic representation of an abstract cosmological concept.

In sum, the temples and monuments such as Borobudur were more than simply places of religious worship – they were centres of demonstrative spiritual superiority. They were a central focus of power and gave a clear message about the position of the ruling monarch. These were the only buildings of stone at that time, and around them grew the courtly complexes that were the centre of society.

HOW WAS IT BUILT?

For Thomas Stamford Raffles, much of this background was simply beyond comprehension. Certainly he could appreciate that a temple of such magnitude was as much a symbol of the ruling hierarchy as of the dominant spiritual belief, but with next to no evidence of who this hierarchy were, Raffles was left very much in the dark. In his extensive *History of Java* he does try to contruct a dynasty, or some kind of history of who ruled when, but we remain vague about this even today. One can well understand, therefore, with so much seemingly unknowable about the temple, that the next questions further baffled him. How had it been constructed? How could the labour have been organized? Who had been the craftsmen? Ironically we probably know more about the pyramids, constructed 3500 years earlier, than we do about Borobudur. In contrast to many other epochs, such as that of the Romans, no dedications were inscribed on the stones that reveal who, when or why? Again one must work with clues and supposition.

Borobudur was mainly constructed of blocks of andesite stone, a common kind of volcanic rock, that can be found throughout the area. Much of central Java is built of andesite. There are many potential quarry sites within a couple of miles of Borobudur, and one can still see big boulders of this material quite nearby. As there have been no quarry sites actually found, it's likely that the stone was picked up in boulders near the river and carved into rough shapes where they lay. Then they would have been transported on bullock carts the few miles to the site of the temple.

Borobudur is made of 1.6 million blocks of this stone. Maybe two or three hundred men were employed at any one time throughout the year on Borobudur, working the stone, levelling the hill, and so on, then carrying out the fine work such as all the decorative carving. If one presumes that much of the exterior was covered with plaster and painted – two other stages of work, which we can't even see now – it is possible that all that work could have been done over a period of 50 to 70 years, even allowing for the probability that it was revised three or four times.

It's probable that people who worked on Borobudur were not paid. As the other shrines of this period, people probably volunteered their labour, as well as stone and other kinds of materials, as a way of earning merit. It doesn't seem as if they were actually forced into working or were required to give any kind of financial support, but rather that in a way this was a labour of faith.

In Southeast Asia, of course, different categories of slavery have existed in the past, but there is no evidence that the treatment of human beings as chattels or property ever existed here. People became so-called slaves for such things as debt, but this basically meant that you entered into a different kind of patron/client relationship with your so-called owner, in which he was actually required to provide for you, making sure that you had food and so on.

The fact that such a building could be made in the absence of slavery is all the more remarkable as a reflection of how coherent a society this was. Wet-rice growing societies need unified planning to administer water supply and drainage. Fields need to be flooded for planting and drained gradually prior to harvesting. So whole areas had to work together. Without that unity, Borobudur would have been impossible.

In addition to those who did the hard labour, the building of the temple must have involved a good number of specialists. There must have been a tremendous demand for artistic skills, for carving wood on houses, palaces and so forth. In central Java there must have been a fairly active artistic community, trained both in pictorial and literary forms. Presumably there were specialist stone masons, too, and the number of temples being built must have kept them in full-time employment.

BUILDING BEGINS

The first block at Borobudur was laid in around AD 780. This was the beginning of the first of many stages.

The first phase created a small building, like a pyramid. Then in a second phase the foundations were widened and made higher. There were five square terraces and a round structure on top. The shape of the temple was to symbolize a mountain – the square terraces representing slopes and the Buddha images in their niches resembling hermits in caves.

Perhaps the most significant
achievement was the ability
of the society at that time to
organize itself to provide 1.6
million blocks of stone.

The original intention for Borobudur seems to have been to build a structure in the shape of a pyramid – but the weight of hundreds of thousands of blocks of andesite proved too much and a giant stone 'girdle' had to be hastily constructed around the edge to prevent complete collapse.

The issue of whether the temple was painted or not is hotly disputed. Certainly no pigmentation has been found but the tropical rains in Java may well have washed any evidence away. It is pure guesswork what a painted Borobudur may have looked like – but it does remain a fascinating possibility.

The number of carvers employed is unknown, of course. But ten or a dozen working steadily would also have needed five, ten, or maybe more years. This work would have been divided between master and apprentice and, indeed, one can see on the lowest level one of the rare inscriptions on Borobudur, which seems to be a note from master to apprentice. It seems that the masters made the outlines and the apprentices did the rest.

In 1885 the 160 lower level reliefs were found by accident. But why had they been covered in the first place? Surely the message contained within them would not have been deliberately obscured? How could the 'lower orders' learn their 'lesson' if they couldn't see them? The 1973–83 UNESCO restoration soon answered these questions. Drillings into the base indicated that the temple is built only partially on a natural hill; it is also built on top of filled-in earth which would very likely have been too insubstantial to support the enormous weight of stone being laid upon it. It would seem that around AD 800 the weight of the upper levels became too great, the foundations weakened and the north face collapsed. It must have been heartbreaking, but the builders had little option but to encircle the temple with a a massive ring of stone to stop the whole thing from crumbling to the ground. Unfortunately that ring of stone, of necessity, covered the lowest level. It also had the effect of widening the temple, so that the original intention of mirroring a steep volcano – a pyramidal form – was compromised.

Borobudur was the first of its type and is still unique in many ways. Although there are several terraced stupas built later than Borobudur – one or two in India, up in the Himalayas, and others, much later, in places like Cambodia and Thailand – Borobudur is the first of these and by far the most elaborate. There is no other example that has this feature of the three round terraces surrounding the central point. There is no other example of perforated stupas anywhere, with or without images inside them.

Nor are there temples in existence that demonstrate this degree of elaborate relief work. In India there are only two or three sites pre-Borobudur which have very many narrative reliefs at all. And at the most these may have fifteen or twenty different scenes; they don't comprise an entire connected narrative. Still less do you have 1500 scenes put together and used to decorate the walls of different ascending levels

Once the the temple was finished – and ready for visitors – it must have been an extraordinary sight. The archaeologist John Miksic conveys the impression it would have made:

If you want to imagine that you're a pilgrim from a thousand years ago seeing Borobudur for the first time, you have to remember several things. You have to remember that you've never seen a stone building in your life. You have to remember that most of the colours around you have always been a single colour – green. You have to remember that you've never seen a very large structure in your life, in fact nothing much bigger than a small hut. If you can hold all those things in your mind and then imagine yourself coming over the rim of the hill for the first time and seeing far off in the distance this vision, shimmering in the sunshine, which is a very large structure of a form you've never seen before with all these spires pointing up, and all the very rectangular structures below it. Imagine too, that it's of many different colours that you've never seen before. It's a gleaming white plaster that has been painted in many different colours, such as reds, yellows and browns, with many different forms that you've never seen before. And then imagine that around it there's a bustling hive of activity, and various other ancillary structures. You could probably be forgiven for thinking that you have stepped into a different world altogether or seen something which has come into this world from somewhere else.

It is quite unlike any other religious monument or building in the world. Its architectural form bears no obvious relationship to any other building that has ever been constructed. It is virtually solid, having no chamber or vault or space inside it. From the moment you arrive at its foot until the moment you reach the top you are on the outside. There is nothing hidden or under a roof. It is totally unique.

CHAPTER 9

WHY WAS IT ABANDONED?

After the beginning of the 10th century no more temples were built in Central Java, and indeed civilization there then seems to have effectively ended. When Raffles in 1815 rediscovered the temple, he had little understanding of such dates but he must have pondered what had caused the monument to be abandoned and left to the jungle. Raffles' view may have been that the arrival of Islam rendered the monument obsolete – he appears not to have considered the possibility of a natural cause.

Slowly even the upper levels would have been obscured and overgrown by ash, dirt and foliage. In many ways, we should be thankful as this has preserved so much of the temple for us to see.

'. . . the sun became obscured, enveloped in a fog. . . This lasted several days, with tremendous explosions, volcanic ash began to fall – the air became darkened by the quantity of falling ashes. [which were eventually] eight inches deep.' These are Raffles' own words describing a volcanic eruption that occurred during his sojourn in Java. The possibility of a similar event a thousand years earlier forcing the cessation of Borobudur's use apparently never occurred to him. Today, however, with the benefit of two more centuries of investigation, we can throw more light on this last great mystery. Borings and soil samples taken over the past few years strongly suggest a major volcanic explosion in AD 928 – about 70 years after the temple had been completed.

John Miksic has been working with volcanologists to see whether there was a volcanic explosion at the time that the temple seems to have been abandoned.

We have been doing some research over the last ten years on the history of volcanism. . .
we have been trying to get as many radiocarbon dates as possible for different eruptions
of Mount Merapi. And as we build up more and more of a database there is a pattern

emerging which does seem to suggest that there was a period of heavy volcanic activity right around the end of the ninth century, around AD 900. Still, it doesn't seem as if the population of central Java was wiped out or decimated. But I can imagine a scenario in which some fairly destructive eruption might have hit the palace or some area which was designated as particularly sacred. And, according to Javanese beliefs and traditions, if some sacred building or a palace is destroyed by a natural event, often it's taken as an omen or a sign that that spot has lost its aura. Also we can see that there is a gradual increase in the trading activity between Java and both the Eastern Archipelago, the Molucca spice islands, and also with the mainland of Asia later on in the tenth century. The location of a palace closer to the coastal areas would have made it easier to control foreign trade, and also might have been seen as propitious. So probably several different factors were involved in the abandonment of Borobudur.

We know that after AD 919 there were no more inscriptions carved in central Java, nor were there any new temples built. There was a gap of 300 years when there were no stone temples built anywhere in Java. Despite a flourishing culture in eastern Java, it was not until the thirteenth century that a revival of stone construction began, but that was several hundred miles to the east of Borobudur. Part of the reason for the low productivity of stone building in eastern Java was simply a lack of materials. The lowlands of the East – where the capital had moved to in AD 929 – had, unlike the vicinity of Borobudur, little available stone.

Even though central Javanese civilization came to an abrupt end, Borobudur was not abandoned overnight. Archaeological evidence suggests that there were at least some people still living in the vicinity of the temple thereafter, probably even still making use of it. Chinese porcelain from the twelfth and thirteenth centuries and Chinese coins from the fourteenth century have been found in the area, which suggests that some visitors continued to visit. The archaeological work done on Borobudur in the early period by the Dutch also suggests that there were probably some visitors to the site as late as the fourteenth century. And, when some restoration work was going on at Borobudur in the 1970s, some ceramics of the Sung dynasty, (which is the period from the tenth to the thirteenth century) were discovered around the foot of the monument. So it seems probable that there were at least a few monks or other devotees sitting around Borobudur long after the centre of Javanese civilization moved east.

The biggest change to Java – and certainly the final event that ruled out any chance of a reawakening of Borobudur – was the arrival of Islam in the fifteenth and sixteenth centuries. Initially the new religion thrived just in the coastal areas, but it gradually spread throughout the island.

People had probably by then lost all remembrance of what Borobudur had been. Volcanic ash had filled the galleries; plants crawled across the reliefs; trees grew around the central stupa. Gradually it began to look like a hill, and was lost.

The
Legacy of
Raffles

'Raffles was an extremely enlightened person for his time … He was the first person who was really willing to acknowledge the fact that the Javanese might have had a civilization in the pre-European phase, and he was able to see that Borobudur was in fact the best firm evidence of that. Borobudur for the first time showed that not just Java but in Southeast Asia there had been a civilization capable of such large-scale unified creative work, so Raffles really deserves a great amount of credit for being able and willing to acknowledge that fact.'

CHAPTER 10

NO LONGER LOST

By 1815 Thomas Stamford Raffles had uncovered and begun some basic restoration of Borobudur. To him it was a fascinating and significant discovery but, back in London, the East India Company was less interested. They had never supported the annexation of Java to their Company's control and had always felt it was a bad financial decision. Raffles had done his best to make profits from trade, particularly in pepper, but his desire to upgrade the social conditions of the Javanese did not come cheap. The East India Company came to the conclusion that Java was simply too much of a drain on resources. In addition, following the Treaty of Vienna in 1815, the Napoleonic Wars came to an end and, as a result, Holland ceased to be French territory. Only two years after news of Borobudur had reached his desk, Raffles received news of a different kind. On 17 October 1815, London took this opportunity to suspend him:

> We have felt much uneasiness lest the new system of Land Revenue so hastily introduced by the Lieutenant-Governor of Java should have served to alienate the minds of numerous individuals... we are decidedly adverse to violent and sudden changes, being convinced that even where the operations of a new system are calculated to improve the condition of the people, much of the intended benefit may be destroyed by an incautious departure from Institutions which have had the sanction of time.

Raffles was journeying through Java at the time, and the news reached him on 18 January 1816.

His possessions ('eastern curiosities and treasures to the amount of thirty tons weight, in upwards of two hundred immense packages') were packed up and, on 25 March 1816, a sad group of friends and associates bade Raffles farewell as he set sail on the ship *Ganges*. Colonel Travers was one of those who saw him off: 'He

was accompanied by all the respectable inhabitants of Batavia, who took leave of him with tears in their eyes, and the chief Chinese and Native inhabitants would not take leave of him till they had seen him on board, when they evinced the deepest grief on taking leave.'

What had Raffles achieved as Lieutenant-Governor of Java? Some argue that a previous Dutch governor, Daendal was in effect more radical than Raffles. The changes he instigated – the building of schools and hospitals – had, it is argued, a more tangible effect. Raffles' land reforms, it is claimed, were more confusing than helpful and he was even implicated in a suspect sale of government land. Whatever Raffles' effect on the island, the British would never get another chance to rule. In August 1816, with Napoleon's French Empire disbanded, Java was returned to the Dutch.

Yet Raffles would not accept defeat and he answered the charges brought against him by a Colonel Gillespie, who had been a rival for power in Java. Gillespie had never been able to accept the 30-year-old commoner as Lieutenant-Governor. He considered himself a much better choice. Raffles, however, successfully had Gillespie's charges dismissed. Indeed Raffles' achievements were beginning to be recognized – in 1817, his great work the *History of Java* was published and, as further proof that he had not completely failed in his efforts, the Prince Regent knighted him in the same year.

In 1818 he was appointed to Benkulu as Lieutenant-Governor of the Company's establishments in West Sumatra. This was a fever-ridden coastline which the East India Company hoped would both supply pepper and prove strategically important on the route to China. Unfortunately it didn't. Raffles did his best, with extra emphasis on spice, sugar and coffee, but it was a harsh life in 'without doubt the most wretched place I ever beheld'.

In 1819, on a small port settlement that no one had paid any attention to, Raffles established a new trading stop that would one day become the world's leading port – Singapore. In 1824, Raffles returned to London, where his most notable act was to found the London Zoological Society.

He never lost his attachment to Java, however. Right up to his untimely death in 1826 (on his probable birthday 6 July), aged just 45, from a brain haemorrhage, he felt justified in placing Java alongside other great ancient cultures. In John Miksic's opinion:

> *Raffles was an extremely enlightened person for his time, and his relationship with*
> *Borobudur exemplifies that. He was the first person who was really willing to acknowledge*

Raffles was distressed at being relieved of his duties as Lieutenant-Governor but the favourable response to his *History of Java* restored his spirits and fortunes.

the fact that the Javanese might have had a civilization in the pre-European phase, and he
was able to see that Borobudur was in fact the best firm evidence of that. Borobudur for the
first time showed that not just Java but in Southeast Asia there had been a civilization
capable of such large-scale unified creative work, so Raffles really deserves a great amount
of credit for being able and willing to acknowledge that fact.

This is a view shared by Nigel Barley: 'I think Borobudur for Raffles brought all sorts of themes together: Java is a civilization, Java has a classical past, Java was a unified state, Java is a place of tremendous technological and artistic sophistication. I think all those came together for Raffles in Borobudur.'

Wurtzburg, Raffles' biographer, wrote: 'Varied scientific interests occupied Raffles' mind, however much he might be beset by official problems. That he had time, let alone any energy, to devote to the exacting requirements of science fills one with amazement. . . Apparently science was so deeply embedded in his mental make-up that he turned to it whenever the slightest opportunity offered, not without effort, but also with a positive sense of relief.'

Raffles' *History of Java* was the first publication to mention Borobudur. One of his colleagues Crawfurd wrote his own book, *History of the Indian Archipelago*, published in 1820, which also mentioned the ruins. Thereafter, with Java back in the hands of the Dutch, years passed with little interest shown in the monuments.

In one sense it was unfortunate that it was a Briton who discovered Borobudur at that time because, with Java's return to the Dutch, the discovery had very little impact. The Dutch on their return continued to have much less interest in ruins than Raffles, and it was not until the 'discovery' of Angkor Wat, in Cambodia, half a century later that international interest began to be shown in Southeast Asia. Angkor Wat had in fact been known for some time – it had been visited by Portuguese, Spanish and even Japanese – but Angkor Wat had at this time the advantage of arousing the interest of a French nation that was colonizing the area. By contrast, after Raffles had gone, the British turned their back on Java and concentrated most of their attention on India and their possessions in the Malay Peninsula.

The absence of such interest internationally was not mirrored within Java. Although the island remained firmly Muslim, by the 1850s, four decades after Raffles, the Javanese were once again conducting rituals on the temple. They carried flowers, incense and candles to the top and prayed at the central stupa for protection and good fortune.

In 1872, the Batavian Society commissioned a complete photographic study, but the photographer, Kinsbergen, found that some of the terrraces on the temple were still covered, with three or four feet of soil and debris. He saw subsidence and rain damage throughout and feared for the temple's stability. His photographs attracted some attention worldwide – the post-impressionist painter Gauguin had one in his studio and incorporated the posture of the seated Buddhas into some of this paintings, such as *Contes Barbares* (1902).

In 1885, the hidden reliefs were discovered and after this, interest in the monument grew. It became clear that the soil that, until Raffles came, had covered the temple had also been protecting it and, now that it was exposed to the elements, there was evidence of a clear deterioration. Indeed the very walls were toppling over. The first serious attempt at restoration began in 1907 under the Dutch engineer Theodore van Erp. The methods he had available were limited, but he tried to secure the monument by effectively drying it out, and using concrete to fill in gaps where rain had accumulated. He also re-laid the circular terraces, and the perforated stupas were largely rebuilt.

Of the 504 Buddha images on Borobudur, almost half are missing their heads. There are also about 50 heads without statues, but even an attempt to match the heads to the bodies by computer proved unsuccessful, as too often the breaks were not clean enough. There are also many museums in the world that have Buddha heads down in their store rooms which probably came from Borobudur. Such heads were easy to dislodge and easy to transport. In the late nineteenth century, the Dutch were trying to foster their relations with Siam and a whole shipload of sculptures from Java, including a lot of statuary from Borobudur, was sent as a gift to their King. Of course Siam, now Thailand, being a Buddhist country, was one where they would have been revered, but sadly, as the boat was leaving for Siam it sank and was lost, so it's quite possible that some heads rest in the Java Sea as well. There are also so many fakes in existence, that the real ones will probably never be identified.

Java remained under Dutch rule until the Japanese occupation from 1942 to 1945. By 1948, the republic of Indonesia had been born. The monument continued to show signs of collapse, and the new Indonesian government knew its lack of funds prevented them from doing much about it. A 'Save Borobudur' appeal in 1968 aroused the interest of UNESCO, drawing contributions from 28 donor countries and much private support, and in the early 1970s the organization initiated a major restoration. It was felt that the monument was in serious danger of collapse. The temple seemed unlikely to survive earthquake or volcanic eruption, and, more mundanely, the huge rains that are common to central Java were undermining the structure's very core.

For over ten years, archaeologists, computer experts, seismologists, physicists, chemists, microbiologists, photographers and meteorologists all worked to ensure that Borobudur would last another thousand years. In the process, over a million of its stones were moved and 170,000 outer stones were numbered, cleaned, treated and replaced.

The temple was completely reopened in 1984 and has become Indonesia's number one attraction, bringing in a million tourists a year, largely Indonesians. Most, of course, are Javanese Muslims as Buddhism is now very much a minority religion in Java. It is one of the five religions officially sanctioned – Islam, Hinduism, Protestantism and Catholicism being the other four – but Buddhists probably make up no more than three or four per cent of the population. Borobudur is considered a national monument, not a religious site. Indeed there is only one Buddhist ceremony a year – Vaisaka. All other communal ceremonies are prohibited. For individual Buddhist pilgrims, however, the temple remains a place of great attraction and spiritual power. Buddhists travel thousands of miles from as far afield as Japan, Tibet and the United States to visit Borobudur.

The large numbers of tourists are causing problems which are hard to avoid – litter, vandalism, over-use. Some experts fear that unless something radical is done, the temple could still collapse. One idea is to cover the whole monument with a see-through dome. The likelihood is that nothing will happen until there is no choice but to act and prevent the temple's demise.

When Raffles discovered the 'lost temple of Java' he brought to light the reality of Southeast Asia's past. The scale and complexity of Borobudur proved, beyond any doubt, that there had once been a civilization of importance, skill and cohesion that had, over a period of decades, worked together to build what remains the largest Buddhist temple in the world. Its 1.6 million blocks, its 1460 reliefs, its stupas and Buddhas all bear testimony to an artistic flowering and cultural achievement that, at a time when Europe was languishing in the Dark Ages,

was in some ways unmatched in human history. Borobudur is unique, in its history, its construction and its use, and we are fortunate that it was a man like Raffles – who thirsted after knowledge – who came across it and treated it with the respect and dignity it deserved.

'To trace the coincidences of the arts, sciences and letters of ancient Java, and

those of Egypt, Greece and Persia, would require more time and more learning than I can command,' wrote Raffles in his *History of Java*. 'Such investigations I must leave to [others], deeming myself fortunate, if in recording their vestiges in the traces of a high state of civilization, to be found in the ruins, languages, poetry, history and institutions of Java, I have succeeded in obtaining any . . . interest. . .'

BIBLIOGRAPHY

Barley, Nigel, *The Duke of Puddle Dock*, Viking, 1991

Bastin, John, *The Native Policies of Sir Thomas Stamford Raffles in Java and Sumatra*, Clarendon Press, 1957

Crawfurd, John, *History of the Indian Archipelago*, Archibald, Constable & Co, 1820

Hall Brierley, Joanna, *The Story of Indonesia's Spice Trade*, OUP, 1994

James, Lawrence, *The Rise and Fall of the British Empire*, Little, Brown, 1994

Ju-Kua, Chau, *Work on the Chinese and Arab Trade in the Twelth and Thirteenth Centuries*, St Petersburg, 1911

Landes, David, *The Wealth and Poverty of Nations*, Little, Brown, 1998

Mackenzie, Lieutenant Colonel, *Narrative of a Journey to Examine the Remains of an Ancient City and Temples at Brambana in Java*, 1819, extract from a manuscript in the Mackenzie collection, The India Office Library, The British Library

Marr, D. G. and Milner, A. C. *Southeast Asia in the Ninth and Tenth Century*, Singapore, 1986

Miksic, John, *Borobudur – Golden Tales of the Buddhas*, Periplus, 1990

Raffles, Lady Sophia, *Memoir of the Life and Public Services of Sir Thomas Stamford Raffles*, London, 1830

Raffles, T.S., extracts from collections of letters and other papers, The British Library

Raffles, T.S., *History of Java*, London, 1817

Soekmono, 'The Restoration of Candi Borobudur', *Indonesia Magazine*, 1982

Tarling, Nicholas, ed., *Cambridge History of Southeast Asia*, vol. 1, CUP, 1992

Teh Gallup, Annabel, *Early Views of Indonesia*, British Library, 1995

Wurtzburg, C.E., *Raffles of the Eastern Isles*, Hodder and Stoughton, 1954

Borobudur – Prayer in Stone, Editions Didier Millet, 1990

The Asiatic Journal, London, 1816

INDEX

PICTURE CREDITS

Ann & Bury Peerless Picture Library: pages 11, 12, 70–1, 80–1, 91, 92,
95, 106–7, 123, 124–5, 131, 138; Antiques Of The Orient, pages 42–3;
Bridgeman Art Library: pages 31, 48, 49, 50, 51, 140–1; Editions Didier
Millet: pages 77, 78; E.T. Archive: page 133; Hulton Getty: page 33;
Images Colour Library: page 20; National Portrait Library: page 26;
Phil Grabsky/Seventh Art Productions: pages 10, 56, 46–7, 64–5,
72, 74, 84–5, 87, 88–9, 96–7, 103, 110–11, 116–17, 136–7;
Yu-Chee Chong Fine Art: pages 28, 31, 38–9, 53, 59, 60–1, 69